# Teach your family the Truth

Building on the basics of the Faith

**Brian Stone**

DayOne

© Day One Publications 2008
First Edition 2008

British Library Cataloguing in Publication Data available

ISBN 978-1-84625-129-0

Published by Day One Publications
Ryelands Road, Leominster, HR6 8NZ

☎ 01568 613 740
FAX: 01568 611 473
email—sales@dayone.co.uk
web site—www.dayone.co.uk

Cover designed by Wayne McMaster and printed by Gutenberg Press, Malta

Dedication

This catechism is dedicated to our grandchildren, with the prayer that they might come to love the Lord with all their heart, soul, mind and strength.

'Train up a child in the way he should go, even when he is old he will not depart from it.'

Proverbs 22:6

# Endorsements

It is obvious that a man must always know, about any given subject, a great deal more than he is going to teach. Brian Stone has proved the benefits and blessings of teaching children Christian truths and values in family worship by means of the Catechism. This book will be a great aid for those whose aim it is to make family worship enjoyable and profitable. From our own personal experience my wife and I have found that teaching children by means of the Children's Catechism has been invaluable, and I am glad to see this publication being made available at this time.

**William G Hughes Pastor, Emmanuel Baptist Church, Coconut Creek, Florida, USA**

Catechising imaginatively, vivaciously and spiritually is a superlative means of grace available for all Christian families. I love the way Brian Stone has put this one together, and I commend it highly.

**Erroll Hulse, Editor, Reformation Today**

I am very pleased that Brian Stone has written this catechism. It has long been needed. Every family should own one in order to improve family worship.

**John Temple, father of four and grandfather to fourteen**

Baptists have a rich heritage of using catechisms to instruct children and new believers. I am delighted that recent years have witnessed a recovery of that heritage. This work by Brian Stone will be a wonderful blessing to parents and children alike who follow its user-friendly plan.

**Tom Ascol, Executive Director of Founders Ministries, Pastor of Grace Baptist Church, Cape Coral, Florida, USA**

# Preface

What you have in your hand is the end result of a family effort. The use of catechisms and confessions has been an invaluable help and tool to us in our family devotions. Over an extended period of time, as we have worked through the *Westminster Shorter Catechism*, we have taken the liberty of rephrasing the questions and answers, not only into modern English, but also at the same time endeavouring to add a Baptist understanding to the questions on baptism.

Questions have been added where we felt the need for further understanding and application. Talking points have been added to encourage further thought and discussion on the questions.

The Scriptural references, which you are encouraged to read, have, by and large, been taken from other catechisms, and they are essential to an understanding of the truth.

The purpose of this current revision is to encourage Christian families in their family devotions with the aid of this catechism. The talking points are there to stimulate discussion and to see what the level of understanding is among your children.

Bible readings have been added which will take you through the Scriptures, in a Scripture reading plan. These readings are not related to the questions and answers.

I said this was a family effort, so I express my deep appreciation to our children, Leanne, Kylie, Clinton and Shanley for many hours of patient and faithful input that has made this possible. Also, I express my deep appreciation to my wife, Judy, for her encouragement and support, not only in this project, but also to the family as a whole. Special thanks, too, to Andrew and Leanne for many hours of typing and editing the manuscript.

May God be glorified as you and your family use this catechism!

Brian Stone

# Acknowledgement

My grateful appreciation to Jim Holmes of Day One, for guiding the process of getting this catechism into print, and for his wisdom and encouragement along the way.

# Outline

Note: The hymns used at the end of each question under 'Something to sing' are taken from the hymnbook *Psalms, Hymns and Songs for Christian Worship* and are reproduced by courtesy of Praise Trust.

# INTRODUCTION

**Q** What is the most important purpose in life for which God has created us?

**A** The most important purpose for which God has created us is to glorify him, worship him and find our joy in him.

*Romans 11:36; 1 Corinthians 10:31; Colossians 3:17; Psalm 73:25–28; Isaiah 61:10*

### SOMETHING TO TALK ABOUT

 ◆ Why should we worship and glorify God?
 ◆ How are we to worship and glorify God?
 ◆ What happens when we do not worship and glorify God?

### BIBLE READING: GOD'S WORK OF CREATION (GENESIS 1)

 ◆ How is man different from all the other animals?
 ◆ After God had created all things, how did he describe it?
 ◆ What did God do on the seventh day?

### ♫ Something to sing ———————————

To God be the glory! Great things he has done;
So loved he the world that he gave us his Son,
Who yielded his life an atonement for sin,
And opened the life-gate that all may go in.

*Praise the Lord, Praise the Lord!*
*Let the earth hear his voice!*
*Praise the Lord, Praise the Lord!*
*Let the people rejoice!*
*O come to the Father, through Jesus the Son,*
*And give him the glory, great things he has done.*
                Frances J. Van Alstyne (676)

**2** **Q** What set of rules has God given to us to show us how we are to worship and glorify him?

**A** The Word of God, which is found in the Old and New Testaments of the Bible, is the only place where we are told how we may worship and glorify God and in so doing, find our joy in him.

*2 Timothy 3:16; Ephesians 2:20; 2 Peter 2:20–21; 1 John 1:3; Revelation 22:18–19*

### SOMETHING TO TALK ABOUT

- Who wrote the Bible?
- Why is the Bible so important?
- Where else are we told what it is that God requires of us?

### ⌂BIBLE READING: ADAM AND EVE (GENESIS 2)

- After God had created Adam and Eve, where did God put them to live?
- What did God give Adam to do in the Garden?
- How did God create Eve?

### ♫ Something to sing

The heavens declare your glory, Lord!
In every star your wisdom shines;
But when we see your holy Word,
We read your name in clearer lines.
Isaac Watts (549)

**3**

**Q** What is the main lesson that the Bible teaches?

**A** The main lesson that the Bible teaches us is what we are to believe about God and what God requires of us.

*2 Timothy 1:13; 2 Timothy 3:16–17; John 20:30–31*

#### SOMETHING TO TALK ABOUT

- ◆ Mention three things the Bible tells us about God.
- ◆ Mention three things the Bible tells us we are to do.

#### BIBLE READING: THE FALL OF MAN (GENESIS 3)

- ◆ What did Adam and Eve do in the Garden that God had forbidden?
- ◆ What did Adam and Eve do after they had sinned?
- ◆ What did God do for them?

### ♪ Something to sing ───────────────

Order my footsteps by your word,
And make my heart sincere;
Let sin have no dominion, Lord,
But keep my conscience clear.

Isaac Watts (560)

◆ Teach your family the Truth

# WHAT GOD IS LIKE

**4**

**Q** Is the Bible trustworthy and reliable in all that it teaches?

**A** Yes. The Bible is absolutely trustworthy and reliable in all that it teaches because it has been given by God himself, and, therefore, no part of it will ever lead us away from God.

*2 Timothy 3:16; 2 Peter 1:20–21; 1 Thessalonians 2:13*

### SOMETHING TO TALK ABOUT

- Why can we trust everything the Bible teaches?
- Is it possible for God to lie?

### BIBLE READING: NOAH AND THE ARK (GENESIS 6)

- Why did God send a flood?
- Why did God choose Noah?
- How many people were saved in the ark?

### ♫ Something to sing

When we walk with the Lord,
In the light of his Word,
What a glory he sheds on our way!
While we do his good will,
He abides with us still,
And with all who will trust and obey!

*Trust and obey! For there's no other way,*
*To be happy in Jesus,*
*But to trust and obey.*

John H. Sammis (853)

12

# 5

**Q** What is God?

**A** God is a Spirit. He has no beginning and no end. He is everlasting, unchangeable, wise, powerful, holy, honest, good and truthful.

*John 4:24; Job 11:7–9; Psalm 90:2; James 1:17; Psalm 147:5; Revelation 4:8; Revelation 15:4; Exodus 34:6–7*

### SOMETHING TO TALK ABOUT

- ◆ Can we see God?
- ◆ What does it mean to be holy?
- ◆ What would happen if God could change?

### 📖 BIBLE READING: GOD'S COVENANT WITH NOAH (GENESIS 9)

- ◆ What did God promise Noah he would never do again?
- ◆ What sign did God give to Noah?
- ◆ What were the names of Noah's sons?

### ♪ Something to sing ────────────────────

Eternal light! Eternal light!
How pure the soul must be,
When, placed within your searching sight,
It shrinks not, but with calm delight
Can face such majesty.
                    Thomas Binney (243)

# 6

**Q** How many Gods are there?

**A** There is only one God who is living and true.

*Deuteronomy 6:14; Jeremiah 10:10; 1 Corinthians 8:4; Isaiah 45:5*

## SOMETHING TO TALK ABOUT

- ◆ What would happen if there were more than one God?
- ◆ How do we know that God is the only true, living God?

## 📖 BIBLE READING: THE TOWER OF BABEL (GENESIS 11)

- ◆ Why did the people build the Tower of Babel?
- ◆ How did God show that he was displeased with what they were doing?
- ◆ Why was God displeased with what they were doing?

## 🎵 Something to sing ———————————

Glory be to God the Father,
Glory be to God the Son,
Glory be to God the Spirit,
Great I AM, the Three-in-One:
Glory, glory,
While eternal ages run!

Horatius Bonar (151)

**7**

**Q** In how many persons does God exist?

**A** God exists in three persons—the Father is God, the Son is God, and the Holy Spirit is God; they are one God, the same in substance, and equal in power and glory.

*Matthew 28:19; 2 Corinthians 13:14; Deuteronomy 6:4; Ephesians 4:5–6; 1 John 5:7*

### SOMETHING TO TALK ABOUT

- Is the Father God?
- Is Jesus Christ God?
- Is the Holy Spirit God?
- Can we fully understand this?
- Why do we believe in the Trinity?

### BIBLE READING: GOD'S CALL TO ABRAHAM (GENESIS 12)

- When Abraham left his own country to go to the land that God had called him to, what was the name of the other man who went with him?
- What was Abraham's wife's name?
- Why did Abraham go to Egypt?

### ♪ Something to sing

Holy, holy, holy, Lord God Almighty!
Early in the morning our song of praise shall be;
'Holy, holy, holy; merciful and mighty,
God in three Persons, glorious Trinity!'
Reginald Heber (159)

# WHAT GOD HAS DONE

**8**

**Q** What are the everlasting purposes of God?

**A** The everlasting purposes of God are: God working out his plans and purposes in a way that everything he has planned from the beginning will happen for his glory.

*Ephesians 1:4, 11; Romans 9:22–23; Romans 8:28; Matthew 10:29; Isaiah 40:13–14*

### SOMETHING TO TALK ABOUT

- ◆ What did God leave out when he planned the world?
- ◆ Did anyone give God advice as to what he should do?
- ◆ When did God make his plan?
- ◆ Can anyone change God's plan and prevent him from doing what he wants to do?

### BIBLE READING: THE STORY OF LOT (GENESIS 19)

- ◆ What was the name of the city in which Lot chose to stay?
- ◆ How would you describe this city?
- ◆ What happened to Lot's wife and why?

### ♪ Something to sing ——————————————

With joy, I welcome, Lord, your right
To every service I can pay;
And call it my supreme delight
To hear your word and to obey.

Philip Doddridge (867)

## 9

**Q** How does God carry out his everlasting purposes?

**A** God carries out his everlasting purposes in creation, and in providing and caring for it.

*Revelation 4:11; Daniel 4:35*

### SOMETHING TO TALK ABOUT

- Who created the world?
- Is there any part of God's creation that he cannot see?
- Is there any part of the world and everything in it that God does not control?
- What does that teach you about God?
- Who is the ruler of the world?

### BIBLE READING: ABRAHAM AND ISAAC (GENESIS 22)

- Why did God say that Abraham should take his son Isaac and sacrifice him?
- When Isaac asked Abraham where the lamb was, what did Abraham say?
- Why did Abraham not sacrifice Isaac?

### ♫ Something to sing ———————————

For the beauty of the earth,
For the beauty of the skies,
For the love which from our birth
Over and around us lies:
Christ our God, to you we raise
This our sacrifice of praise.
Folliott Sandford Pierpoint (206)

# GOD'S CREATION

## 10

**Q** What is creation?

**A** Creation is God making everything out of nothing in six days by the powerful word that he spoke, and everything he created was very good.

*Genesis 1:1; Hebrews 11:3; Genesis 1:31*

#### SOMETHING TO TALK ABOUT

- ◆ Who created all things?
- ◆ What did God use to create the world?
- ◆ How long did God take to create the world?
- ◆ In what condition did God create everything?
- ◆ Why is the world not perfect today?

#### 📖 BIBLE READING: ISAAC AND REBEKAH (GENESIS 24)

- ◆ What was the one thing Abraham wanted for Isaac before he died?
- ◆ The servant whom Abraham sent prayed a special prayer. Did the Lord answer his prayer?
- ◆ What was the name of Isaac's wife?

#### 🎵 Something to sing ────────────────

*All things bright and beautiful,*
*All creatures great and small,*
*All things wise and wonderful,*
*The Lord God made them all.*

Each little flower that opens,
Each little bird that sings,
He made their glowing colours,
He made their tiny wings.

Cecil Frances Alexander (204, verse 1)

**11**

**Q** How did God create Adam and Eve?

**A** God created Adam and Eve in his own likeness, perfect and without sin, knowing how to please God and how to rule over the world he had made.

*Genesis 1:26–27; Colossians 3:10; Ephesians 4:24; Genesis 1:28*

SOMETHING TO TALK ABOUT

◆ Who created Adam and Eve?
◆ Why did God make you?
◆ On what day did God create Adam?
◆ What is the difference between us, today, and Adam, when God created him?

**BIBLE READING: JACOB'S VISION (GENESIS 28)**

◆ What did Jacob see in the dream that he had?
◆ What did Jacob call the place where he had the dream?
◆ What promise did Jacob make to God?

♫ **Something to sing**

*All things bright and beautiful,*
*All creatures great and small,*
*All things wise and wonderful,*
*The Lord God made them all.*

He gave us eyes to see them,
And lips that we might tell
How great is God Almighty
Who has made all things well.

Cecil Frances Alexander (204, verse 4)

# GOD'S PROVIDENCE

**12**

**Q** What is God's providence?

**A** God's providence is his keeping, caring for, and controlling everything he has made in such a way that, in the end, everything he had planned from the beginning will be as he intended.

*Psalm 145:17; Psalm 104:24; Isaiah 28:29; Hebrews 1:8; Psalm 103:19; Matthew 10:29–31*

## SOMETHING TO TALK ABOUT

- What are some of the things God controls?
- What would happen if God were not in control?
- What has happened to things which God has given to man to look after?

## BIBLE READING: JACOB WRESTLES WITH AN ANGEL (GENESIS 32)

- How did Jacob feel when he heard that his brother Esau was coming to meet him?
- Why did he react in this way?
- What happened to Jacob that night?

## ♫ Something to sing

My God, I thank you that you made the earth so bright,
So full of splendour and of joy, beauty and light;
So many glorious things are here, noble and right.

Adelaide A. Procter (209)

**13**

**Q** What special act of providence did God show towards Adam, whom he created?

**A** After God created Adam, he entered into an agreement with him in which he promised to give him everlasting life, on condition that he obeyed God perfectly and that he did not eat of the tree of knowledge of good and evil. If he did eat of this tree, he would die.

*Genesis 2:16–17; Galatians 3:12*

### SOMETHING TO TALK ABOUT

- An agreement is a covenant made between two or more people. In this covenant (agreement) that God made with Adam, what did Adam have to do?
- What did God promise to give Adam in this covenant if he was obedient?
- What did God say he would do if Adam was disobedient?

### 📖 BIBLE READING: JOSEPH AND HIS BROTHERS (GENESIS 37)

- Why did his brothers sell Joseph?
- To whom was he sold?
- What was the name of the brother who suggested that they sell Joseph?

### 🎵 Something to sing

My Lord, I did not choose you,
For that could never be;
This heart would still refuse you
Had you not chosen me:
You took the sin that stained me,
You cleansed and made me new;
For you of old ordained me
That I should live to you.

Josiah Conder (691)

# HOW MAN SINNED

**14**

**Q** Did our first parents remain as God created them?

**A** No, our first parents, who were created by God with their own free wills, chose to disobey God, and, in so doing, no longer remained in the perfect condition in which God created them.

*Genesis 3:6–8, 13; Ecclesiastes 7:29; Deuteronomy 30:19; Romans 3:12*

### SOMETHING TO TALK ABOUT

- ◆ Who were our first parents?
- ◆ How would you describe their original condition in which God created them?
- ◆ What happened between God and our first parents after they had disobeyed God?

### 📖 BIBLE READING: JOSEPH INTERPRETS PHARAOH'S DREAMS (GENESIS 41)

- ◆ To whom was Joseph sold as a slave in Egypt?
- ◆ Why was he put in prison?
- ◆ Who was with Joseph in prison? (See verse 21.)

### ♫ Something to sing —————————————————

Come, you souls by sin afflicted,
Fruitless sorrow bows you down;
By the broken law convicted,
Through the cross behold the crown;
Look to Jesus,
Look to Jesus,
Look to Jesus,
Mercy flows through him alone,
Mercy flows through him alone.

Joseph Swain (666)

# 15

**Q** What is sin?

**A** Sin is not only doing what God forbids, but also not doing what God commands.

*1 John 3:4; Romans 3:20; James 2:9–11*

#### SOMETHING TO TALK ABOUT

- ◆ What are the two kinds of sin of which we can be guilty?
- ◆ Mention two from each category.
- ◆ Where are we told what God forbids and what God commands?
- ◆ Read Exodus 20:1–17 and list the things that God says we should and should not do.

#### 📖 BIBLE READING: THE BIRTH OF MOSES AND HIS EARLY LIFE (EXODUS 2)

- ◆ Why was Moses hidden in the reeds along the River Nile?
- ◆ When Pharaoh's daughter found him, whom did she send for in order to look after Moses?
- ◆ Why did Moses flee from Egypt?

### ♫ Something to sing ——————————————

The gospel of your grace
My stubborn heart has won,
For God so loved the world
He gave his only Son
So that whoever will believe
Shall everlasting life receive!

The soul that sins shall die!
My awful doom I heard;
I was for ever lost
But for your gracious word,
Which says, whoever will believe
Shall everlasting life receive!

Arthur T. Pierson (706)

# 16

**Q** What was the sin that resulted in our first parents falling from their original condition?

**A** The sin resulting in our first parents falling from their original condition was that they ate of the forbidden fruit.

*Genesis 3:6–8, 11*

## SOMETHING TO TALK ABOUT

- ◆ What was so terrible about the sin of Adam and Eve?
- ◆ Give some reasons why this sin was so displeasing to God.
- ◆ When they sinned, they showed that they did not trust the Word of God. Is this always the case with sin?

## BIBLE READING: THE BURNING BUSH (EXODUS 3)

- ◆ What was so strange about the burning bush that Moses saw?
- ◆ Why was Moses told to take off his shoes?
- ◆ What did God tell Moses to do?

## ♫ Something to sing

Not what these hands have done
Can save this guilty soul,
And nothing that this flesh has borne
Can make my spirit whole.

Your work alone, O Christ,
Can ease this weight of sin;
Your blood alone, O Lamb of God,
Can give me peace within.

Horatius Bonar (701, verses 1 and 3)

# THE CONSEQUENCES OF MAN'S SIN

**17**

**Q** Were all people affected by the sin of Adam?

**A** Yes. Everyone born in the natural way by their parents has been affected by Adam's sin, as he was acting as the representative of all people.

*Genesis 1:28; Genesis 2:16–17; Romans 5:12, 18–19; 1 Corinthians 15:21–22*

### SOMETHING TO TALK ABOUT

- ◆ Who was affected as a result of Adam's sin? Why?
- ◆ Who was not affected by Adam's sin when he was born? Why?

### BIBLE READING: THE PLAGUES IN EGYPT (EXODUS 7–11)

- ◆ How many plagues did God send on the Egyptians?
- ◆ Why did God send the plagues?
- ◆ What was the last plague that God sent?

## ♪ Something to sing

A debtor to mercy alone,
Of covenant mercy I sing;
Nor fear, with your righteousness on,
My person and offering to bring:
The terrors of law and of God
With me can have nothing to do;
My Saviour's obedience and blood
Hide all my transgressions from view.

Augustus M. Toplady (773)

**18** **Q** What was the result of man's falling into sin?

**A** The result of man's falling into sin was that he fell into a state of sin and misery.

*Romans 3:10–18; Romans 5:12*

### SOMETHING TO TALK ABOUT

- From Romans 3:10–18, make a list of the results of the fall.
- To see what Adam was like before he sinned, make a list of the opposites of the list above.
- What was the worst result of Adam's sin?

### BIBLE READING: THE FIRST PASSOVER (EXODUS 12)

- What animal did God say had to be killed?
- What were the people to do with the blood?
- What promise did God give to those who did what he said?

### ♪ Something to sing ————————————

Long my imprisoned spirit lay
Fast bound in sin and nature's night:
Then shone your glorious gospel ray;
I woke! The dungeon flamed with light!
My chains fell off; my heart was new,
I rose, went forth and followed you!
My chains fell off; my heart was new,
I rose, went forth and followed you!
Charles Wesley (776, verse 4)

# 19

**Q** What is the sinfulness of man's fallen condition?

**A** The sinfulness of man's fallen condition is that he has inherited a sinful nature, which means that the guilt of Adam's sin has resulted in his no longer being righteous, good and pure, and it is from this sinful nature that acts of disobedience come.

*Romans 3:10; Romans 5:10–20; Ephesians 2:1–3; James 1:14–15; Matthew 15:19; Psalm 51:5*

### SOMETHING TO TALK ABOUT

- Why are we born with a sinful nature?
- How do we know that man has a sinful nature?
- Who is responsible for the sins we commit?

### BIBLE READING: CROSSING THE RED SEA (EXODUS 14)

- Why did Pharaoh chase Moses and the Israelites?
- What miracle did God perform to save the Israelites?
- What happened to Pharaoh and the Egyptians?

### ♪ Something to sing

And can it be that I should gain
An interest in the Saviour's blood?
Died he for me, who caused his pain?
For me, who him to death pursued?
Amazing love! How can it be
That you, my God, should die for me?
Amazing love! How can it be
That you, my God, should die for me?

Charles Wesley (776, verse 1)

## 20

**Q** What is the miserable result of man's original sin?

**A** The result of man's original sin is that he lost fellowship with God, he came under God's anger and curse, and was made subject to the unhappiness of life and death and to the pains of hell for ever.

*Genesis 3:8, 10, 17, 24; Ephesians 2:1–3; Galatians 3:10; Romans 6:23; Matthew 25:41, 46; Ezekiel 18:4; Isaiah 59:2*

### SOMETHING TO TALK ABOUT

- Who has lost fellowship with God?
- Who has come under God's anger and curse?
- Who will experience the pains of hell for ever?
- How do we know that there really is a hell?

### BIBLE READING: MANNA AND QUAIL (EXODUS 16)

- Where did the Israelites get their food from in the wilderness?
- How much food were they to collect each day, and how much on the Sabbath day?
- What happened to the food if the people collected too much?

### ♪ Something to sing

Today your mercy calls us
To wash away our sin,
However great our trespass,
Whatever we have been;
However long from mercy
Our hearts have turned away,
Your blood, O Christ, can cleanse us
And set us free today.

Oswald Allen (677)

# SALVATION

**21**

**Q** Did God leave all mankind to die in the misery of sin?

**A** From before the beginning of the world, and only because it pleased God, he chose some to have everlasting life; this he did by entering into a covenant of grace with Jesus Christ, his eternal Son, on whose behalf he would free those whom he had chosen from the misery of sin and bring them to salvation through a Saviour.

*Genesis 3:15; Ephesians 1:4; Romans 3:20–22; Galatians 3:21–22; 2 Timothy 1:9*

### SOMETHING TO TALK ABOUT

- ◆ Why did God make a covenant of grace?
- ◆ What would have happened to us all if God had not done so?
- ◆ Who are the ones who benefit from this covenant of grace?

### BIBLE READING: WATER FROM THE ROCK (EXODUS 17)

- ◆ Were the Israelites glad to be out of Egypt?
- ◆ What made them dissatisfied at this stage?
- ◆ How did God give them what they wanted?

### ♫ Something to sing

Eternity will not erase
My name from the palms of his hands;
In marks of indelible grace
Impressed on his heart it remains:
Yes, I to the end shall endure,
As sure as the promise is given;
More happy, but not more secure,
The glorified spirits in heaven.

Augustus M. Toplady (773, verse 3)

**22**

**Q** Who is the Saviour of those whom God has chosen?

**A** The only Saviour of those whom God has chosen is the Lord Jesus Christ, who, as the eternal Son of God, became man and continues to be God and man in one person for ever.

*John 1:14; Acts 4:12; Galatians 4:4; 1 Timothy 2:5–6; Hebrews 2:14; Hebrews 7:24; Hebrews 13:8*

#### SOMETHING TO TALK ABOUT

- Besides the Lord Jesus Christ, what other ways are there of being saved?
- From what have we been saved? (See Question 20.)
- Why is Jesus Christ the only Saviour?
- How do we know that Jesus Christ is God?

#### BIBLE READING: THE TEN COMMANDMENTS (EXODUS 20)

- What was the first commandment that God gave to Moses?
- What was the fifth commandment that God gave to Moses?
- How did God give these commandments to Moses, and on what were they written?

### ♫ Something to sing

Your mercy, my God, is the theme of my song,
The joy of my heart, and the boast of my tongue;
Your free grace alone, from the first to the last,
Has won my affections, and bound my soul fast.

Great Father of mercies, your goodness I own,
And the covenant love of your crucified Son;
All to the Spirit, whose whisper divine
Seals mercy and pardon and righteousness mine.

J. S. in Gospel Magazine (273, verses 1 and 5)

**23**

**Q** How did Jesus Christ, being the Son of God, become man?

**A** Jesus Christ became man by taking on a true human body; this came about as a result of the miraculous work of the Holy Spirit in the womb of the Virgin Mary, who gave birth to Jesus Christ, and yet he was born without sin.

*Hebrews 2:14, 16; Hebrews 10:5; Luke 1:27, 31, 35, 42; Galatians 4:4; Hebrews 4:15; Hebrews 7:26*

### SOMETHING TO TALK ABOUT

- ◆ Was the birth of Jesus Christ the same as any other birth?
- ◆ Mention two ways in which the birth of Christ was similar, and two ways in which it was different from that of your own birth.
- ◆ Has there ever been another birth like that of Jesus Christ?

### BIBLE READING: THE GOLDEN CALF (EXODUS 32)

- ◆ Why did Aaron build a golden calf?
- ◆ Which commandment was he breaking?
- ◆ What did God do to the people because of this?

### ♫ Something to sing

He left his Father's throne above—
So free, so infinite his grace—
Humbled himself in all his love
And bled for Adam's helpless race.
What mercy this, immense and free,
For, O my God, it found out me!
What mercy this, immense and free,
For, O my God, it found out me!

Charles Wesley (776, verse 3)

# THE WORK OF CHRIST IN SALVATION

**24**

**Q** As our Saviour, what three positions or functions does Christ occupy?

**A** As our Saviour, Christ has the position (office) of Prophet, Priest and King, and these positions he occupies while on earth and in heaven.

*Acts 3:21–22; Hebrews 12:25; 2 Corinthians 13:3; Hebrews 5:5–7; Hebrews 7:25; Psalm 2:6–11; Isaiah 9:6–7; Matthew 21:5*

### SOMETHING TO TALK ABOUT

◆ Is there anyone else in the Bible who was a prophet, priest and king?
◆ Mention one prophet, one priest and one king in the Bible.
◆ Was any of them perfect?

### 📖BIBLE READING: THE DAY OF THE ATONEMENT (LEVITICUS 16)

◆ Was Aaron allowed to go into God's presence whenever he felt like it?
◆ What were some of the things that God said he had to do before going into God's presence?
◆ What does this chapter teach us?

### ♬ Something to sing —————————————————————

Arise, my soul, arise,
Shake off your guilty fears;
The perfect sacrifice
On my behalf appears:
My guarantor in heaven stands,
My name is written on his hands.

He ever lives above
For me to intercede,
His all-redeeming love,
His precious blood, to plead;
His blood atoned for every race
And sprinkles now the throne of grace.

Charles Wesley (502, verses 1 and 2)

**25**

**Q** How does Christ carry out his office as a Prophet?

**A** As a Prophet, Christ reveals God's will to us for our salvation and this he does through his Word and by his Spirit.

*John 1:18; 1 Peter 1:10–12; John 15:15; John 20:31*

SOMETHING TO TALK ABOUT

* What is the work of a prophet?
* Mention at least three things that Christ, who is our Prophet, has told us in the Bible.

**BIBLE READING: EXPLORING THE LAND OF CANAAN (NUMBERS 13–14)**

* How many spies did Moses send to spy out the land of Canaan?
* How many believed that God would help them conquer the land?
* What was God's punishment on those who did not believe God would help them?

♪ **Something to sing** ————————————————

Divine Instructor, gracious Lord
Be now and ever near;
Teach me to love your sacred word
And view my Saviour there.

Anne Steele (545, verse 6)

## 26

**Q** How does Christ carry out his office as a Priest?

**A** As a Priest, Christ offers himself as a sacrifice to satisfy God's perfect standard and, in so doing, to make peace between God and us, and he continually speaks to God on our behalf.

*Hebrews 9:14, 28; Hebrews 2:17; Hebrews 7:24–25*

### SOMETHING TO TALK ABOUT

+ What is the work of a Priest?
+ Mention two things that Christ, as our Priest, has done for us.

### BIBLE READING: THE BRONZE SNAKE (NUMBERS 21)

+ Why did God send snakes among the people of Israel?
+ What did God tell Moses to do, so that the people would not die?
+ After the people were bitten, who were the ones that lived?

### ♫ Something to sing

Before the throne of God above
I have a strong, a perfect plea,
A great high priest, whose name is love,
Who ever lives and pleads for me.
My name is written on his hands,
My name is hidden in his heart;
I know that while in heaven he stands
No power can force me to depart,
No power can force me to depart.
Charitie L. Bancroft (503)

## 27

**Q** How does Christ carry out his office as a King?

**A** As a King, Christ brings us under his authority by ruling over us, defending us, and by controlling and conquering all his enemies and ours.

*Acts 15:14–16; Isaiah 33:22; Isaiah 32:1–2;*
*1 Corinthians 15:25*

### SOMETHING TO TALK ABOUT

- ◆ What is the work of a King?
- ◆ Mention three things that Christ, as our King, has done (or is doing) for us.

### 📖 BIBLE READING: BALAAM AND THE DONKEY (NUMBERS 22)

- ◆ Who was Balak and who was Balaam?
- ◆ What did Balaam's donkey see which Balaam could not see?
- ◆ What was the miracle that God performed in this chapter?

### ♪ Something to sing

Lamb of God, you are now seated
High upon your Father's throne,
All your gracious work completed,
All your mighty victory won;
Every knee in heaven is bending
To the Lamb for sinners slain;
All sing forth his unending—
'Worthy is the Lamb to reign!'
                    James G. Deck (492)

## 28

**Q** How was Christ humiliated?

**A** Christ was humiliated by being born, as a man, into a poor family, was made subject to the law of God, experienced the sufferings and miseries of this life, the anger of God, the curse of death on a cross, and was buried and remained under the power of death for a time.

*Luke 2:7; Galatians 4:4; Hebrews 12:2–3; Isaiah 53:2–3; Luke 22; Matthew 27:46; Philippians 2:8; 1 Corinthians 15:3; Acts 2:24–31*

### SOMETHING TO TALK ABOUT

- Was it absolutely necessary for Christ to be born into this world, and, if so, why?
- What do you think was the most difficult part of Christ's humiliation?

### 📖 BIBLE READING: THE DEATH OF MOSES (DEUTERONOMY 34)

- Did Moses ever enter the promised land of Canaan that God said he would give to the children of Israel?
- When Moses died, who buried him?
- Who continued to lead the Children of Israel after Moses' death?

### ♫ Something to sing —————————————————

Behold, the great Creator makes
Himself a house of clay;
A robe of human form he takes
For ever from this day.

This wonder all the world amazed
And shook the starry frame;
The hosts of heaven stood and gazed,
Then blessed the Saviour's name.

Thomas Pestel (355)

**29 Q** How is Christ honoured?

**A** Christ is honoured (exalted) by God raising him from the dead on the third day, by his going up (ascending) into heaven, by his sitting at the right hand of God, the Father, and in his coming to judge the world at the end of time.

*1 Corinthians 15:4; Mark 16:19; Acts 1:11; Acts 17:31; Philippians 2:9–11*

#### Something to talk about

◆ Why was it necessary for Christ to be raised from the dead?
◆ Mention three ways in which God has honoured Christ.

#### BIBLE READING: Rahab and the spies (Joshua 2)

◆ How many spies did Joshua send to look over the land, and especially to look over Jericho?
◆ Who was the one who protected them in her home?
◆ What promise did the spies give her when they left?

#### ♪ Something to sing —————————————

Come, let us join our cheerful songs
With angels round the throne;
Ten thousand thousand are their tongues,
But all their joys are one.

'Worthy the Lamb who died,' they cry,
'To be exalted thus!'
'Worthy the Lamb,' our lips reply,
'For he was slain for us!'

Isaac Watts (300, verses 1 and 2)

# THE WORK OF THE HOLY SPIRIT IN SALVATION

**30**

**Q** How are we to take part in the salvation (redemption) which Christ, our Saviour bought (purchased) for us?

**A** We are able to take part in this salvation bought by Christ when the Holy Spirit makes us alive to receive it, (that is, effectively applies it to us).

*John 1:11–12; Titus 3:5–6*

### SOMETHING TO TALK ABOUT

- ◆ Are we able to be saved without the Holy Spirit?
- ◆ Why is it necessary for the Holy Spirit to make us alive?

### BIBLE READING: THE FALL OF JERICHO (JOSHUA 6)

- ◆ What great miracle did God perform in this chapter?
- ◆ While all the people of Jericho were destroyed, there was one family that was saved; who was that family?
- ◆ Why was this family saved?

### ♫ Something to sing ————————————————

O, precious words that Jesus said!—
All those who come to me,
I will not ever turn away,
Whoever they may be.
O, precious words that Jesus said!—
Behold, I am the door;
And all who enter in by me
Have life for evermore.

Frances J. van Alstyne (670)

## 31

**Q** How does the Holy Spirit apply this salvation that Christ bought for us?

**A** The Holy Spirit applies this salvation that Christ has bought for us, by enabling us to believe the gospel and repent of our sin, and in so doing, making us God's children.

*Ephesians 1:13–14; John 6:37–39; Ephesians 2:8; Ephesians 3:17; 1 Corinthians 1:9*

### SOMETHING TO TALK ABOUT

- ◆ Why is it necessary for the Holy Spirit to help us believe?
- ◆ What does he enable us to believe concerning Christ?

### 📖 BIBLE READING: ACHAN'S SIN (JOSHUA 7)

- ◆ What happened to Joshua's men when they went to fight against the city of Ai?
- ◆ What was the cause of the problem?
- ◆ What happened to Achan and his family who had been disobedient to God?

### 🎵 Something to sing ——————————————

Spirit of faith, come down,
Reveal the things of God
And make to us the Godhead known
And point to Jesus' blood.
Your work the blood to apply:
O give us eyes to see
That he who did for sinners die
Has surely died for me.

Charles Wesley (523)

**32**

**Q** What made God's call real (effective) in our lives?

**A** God's call is made real (effective) in our lives by the work of God's Spirit, who convinces us that we are sinful and who enables us to understand the purpose and work of Christ and who changes our wills so as to bring us to the place where we recognize our need to believe and receive Jesus Christ, who is freely offered in the gospel.

*2 Timothy 1:9; 2 Thessalonians 2:13–14; Acts 2:37; Acts 26:18; Ezekiel 36:26–27; John 6:44–45; Philippians 2:13*

### SOMETHING TO TALK ABOUT

◆ If the Holy Spirit did not convince us that we are sinful, would we ever come to Christ by our own choice?
◆ What do we understand by the word 'gospel'?

### BIBLE READING: THE SUN STANDS STILL (JOSHUA 10)

◆ What two miracles did God perform in this chapter?
◆ Why was it necessary for God to do this?
◆ What do we learn about God from this chapter?

## ♫ Something to sing —————————————————

My Lord, I did not choose you,
For that could never be;
This heart would still refuse you
Had you not chosen me:
You took the sin that stained me,
You cleansed and made me new;
For you of old ordained me
That I should live for you.

Josiah Conder (691)

# THE BENEFITS OF SALVATION THAT WE ENJOY IN THIS LIFE

**33**

**Q** What benefits do we, who are effectively called by God, experience in this life?

**A** The benefits of being effectively called by God are that, in this life, he justifies, adopts and sanctifies us, along with the blessings that flow from these.

*Romans 8:30; Ephesians 1:5; 1 Corinthians 1:26, 30*

### SOMETHING TO TALK ABOUT

◆ What does it mean to be 'effectively called' by God?

### BIBLE READING: GOD'S CALL TO GIDEON (JUDGES 6)

◆ Why did God give the children of Israel a man called Gideon?
◆ God performed another two miracles in this chapter. What were they?
◆ Gideon asked God for a sign to show him that God had chosen him. What was it?

### ♪ Something to sing

How vast the benefits divine
Which we in Christ possess!
We are redeemed from sin and shame
And called to holiness.
Not for the works that we have done—
All these to him are owed;
But he of his electing love
Salvation has bestowed.

Augustus M. Toplady and Dewey Westra (711)

## 34

**Q** What is justification?

**A** Justification is an act of God's goodness (free grace), by which he forgives all our sins, accepts us as righteous in his sight, treats us as though we had never sinned, and all this he does on the basis that Christ died; he died on our behalf, and this justification is received by faith alone.

*Romans 3:24–25; Romans 4:6–7; 2 Corinthians 5:19–21; Romans 5:17–19; Galatians 2:16; Philippians 3:9*

### SOMETHING TO TALK ABOUT

- ◆ Why is justification spoken of as an act of God's goodness?
- ◆ Do we deserve to be justified?
- ◆ What are we to do to receive justification?
- ◆ What does it mean to be 'treated as though we had never sinned'?

### 📖 BIBLE READING: GIDEON AND THE MIDIANITES (JUDGES 7)

- ◆ When Gideon went to fight against the Midianites, what was the first thing that God said to him?
- ◆ In the end, how many men did Gideon take with him?
- ◆ Why did God want Gideon to have so few soldiers against so many?

### 🎵 Something to sing ——————————————

O teach me, Lord, its meaning
The cross uplifted high,
With one, the Man of sorrows,
Condemned to bleed and die!
O teach me what it cost you
To make a sinner whole;
And teach me, Saviour, teach me
The value of a soul.

Lucy A. Bennett (440)

**35 Q** What is adoption?

**A** Adoption is an act of God's free grace, by which we become the children of God with all the rights and privileges that God gives to his children.

*1 John 3:1; John 1:12; Romans 8:17*

#### SOMETHING TO TALK ABOUT

- Do we automatically become the children of God when we are born into this world?
- What are some of the rights and privileges that God's children enjoy?

#### 📖 BIBLE READING: SAMSON AND DELILAH (JUDGES 16)

- How do we know that Delilah did not really love Samson?
- What did Delilah do to Samson so that he lost his strength?
- How did Samson die?

#### ♪ Something to sing ——————————————

Behold the amazing gift of love
The Father has bestowed
On us, the sinful sons of men,
To call us sons of God!

High is the rank we now possess,
But higher we shall rise;
Though what we shall hereafter be
Is hidden from our eyes.

Scottish paraphrases based on Isaac Watts (780, verses 1 and 3)

# 36

**Q** What is sanctification?

**A** Sanctification is a work of God's free grace in which he makes us holy in heart and life (conduct) and in so doing, we are enabled more and more to stop sinning and to live a life that is pleasing to God.

*2 Thessalonians 2:13; Ephesians 4:23–24; Romans 6:4, 6; Romans 8:1*

## SOMETHING TO TALK ABOUT

- ◆ What kind of life does God enable us to live?
- ◆ How do we know whether or not our lives are pleasing to God?
- ◆ Do you think that we can ever come to that place in this life where we are perfect in all that we say and do?

## 📖 BIBLE READING: RUTH AND NAOMI (RUTH 1)

- ◆ What were Ruth and Orpah to Naomi?
- ◆ When Naomi returned to Bethlehem, who went with her?
- ◆ Why was Naomi sad when she went back to her land?

## 🎵 Something to sing ————————————————

More about Jesus would I know,
More of his grace to others show,
More of his saving fulness see,
More of his love—who died for me.

*More, more about Jesus,*
*More, more about Jesus,*
*More of his saving fulness see,*
*More of his love who died for me.*
Eliza E. Hewitt (733)

**37**

**Q** What are the benefits in this life that result from justification, adoption, and sanctification?

**A** The benefits in this life that result from justification, adoption and sanctification are: the assurance of God's love, peace of conscience, joy in the Holy Spirit, a growing understanding of God's grace, and a desire to live a life which is pleasing to God.

*Romans 5:1–2, 5; Romans 14:17; Proverbs 4:18; 1 John 5:13; 1 Peter 1:5*

#### SOMETHING TO TALK ABOUT

- ♦ Can we be justified without being adopted into the family of God?
- ♦ Can we be adopted by God into his family and then later be put out of God's family?

#### ⌖BIBLE READING: RUTH AND BOAZ (RUTH 2)

- ♦ When Naomi and Ruth returned, what did Ruth do to get food?
- ♦ To whose field did she go to gather food?
- ♦ What happened to Ruth as a result of her going to that particular field?

### ♫ Something to sing————————————

O Christ, in you my soul has found
And found in you alone,
The peace that I had sought so long,
The joy till now unknown.

*Now none but Christ can satisfy,*
*No other name so true;*
*There's love and life and lasting joy,*
*Lord Jesus, found in you.*

Anon (782)

# THE BENEFITS OF SALVATION THAT WE ENJOY AFTER DEATH

**38**

**Q** When believers die, what benefits do they receive from Christ?

**A** The benefits that believers receive when they die are that they will be made perfectly holy and will immediately pass into the glories of heaven.

*Hebrews 12:28; 2 Corinthians 5:1, 6, 8; Philippians 1:23; Luke 23:43; 1 Thessalonians 4:14; Isaiah 57:2; Job 19:26–27*

### SOMETHING TO TALK ABOUT

* Is death for a Christian and a non-Christian the same kind of experience?
* What do you think 'perfectly holy' means?

### BIBLE READING: THE BIRTH OF SAMUEL (1 SAMUEL 1)

* What was the prayer that Hannah prayed?
* Did God hear and answer this prayer?
* Did Hannah keep the promise that she had made to God?

### ♪ Something to sing

When I tread the verge of Jordan,
Bid my anxious fears subside;
Death of death, and hell's destruction,
Land me safe on Canaan's side:
Songs of praises, songs of praises,
I will ever sing to you,
I will ever sing to you.

William Williams (868, verse 3)

## 39

**Q** When Christ returns, what benefits will believers receive?

**A** The benefits that believers will receive at Christ's return are that they will be publicly acknowledged as the sons and daughters of God, they will be declared not guilty on the day of judgement, and will enjoy the glories of heaven.

*1 Corinthians 15:43; Matthew 25:23; 1 John 3:2; 1 Corinthians 13:12; 1 Thessalonians 4:17–18*

### SOMETHING TO TALK ABOUT

◆ When will Christ return?
◆ How will it be possible for believers to be declared 'not guilty' on the day of judgement?
◆ If you knew that Jesus Christ was going to return at twelve o'clock tomorrow, what would you do?

### BIBLE READING: THE LORD CALLS SAMUEL (1 SAMUEL 3)

◆ Who was Samuel staying with as he grew up in the temple?
◆ When God spoke to Samuel, who did he think it was who was calling him?
◆ Was God's vision to Samuel good news or bad news for Eli?

### ♪ Something to sing ——————————————

Hear the Church triumphant singing,
'Worthy the Lamb!'
Highest heaven with praises ringing,
'Worthy the Lamb!'
Thrones and powers before him bending,
Odours sweet with voice ascending
Swell the chorus never-ending:
'Worthy the Lamb!'
John Kent (967)

## 40

**Q** What will happen to the wicked on the day of judgement?

**A** On the day of judgement the wicked will be punished by God by being sent to hell with the devil and his angels for ever and ever (that is, for all eternity).

*John 5:28–29; Daniel 12:2; 2 Thessalonians 1:8–9; Matthew 25:41, 46*

### SOMETHING TO TALK ABOUT

- Will the wicked have another opportunity to be saved after Christ's return?
- What do you think the most terrible part of hell will be?

### 📖 BIBLE READING: SAMUEL ANOINTS SAUL AS KING (1 SAMUEL 9–10)

- Why was Saul looking for Samuel; what did he want Samuel to do for him?
- What did Samuel do to Saul, which Saul was not expecting?
- When the people wanted to make Saul king over Israel, why could they not find him?

### ♫ Something to sing ———————————

Jesus your blood and righteousness
My beauty are, my glorious dress;
Mid burning worlds, in these arrayed,
With joy I shall life up my head.

Bold shall I stand on your great day
And none condemn me, try who may;
Fully absolved by you I am
From sin and fear, from guilt and shame.

Nicolaus L. Von Zinzendorf (778, verses 1 and 2)

# THE LAW OF GOD

**41**

**Q** What duty does God require of man?

**A** The duty that God requires of man is that he obeys what God has written (revealed) in his Word.

*Micah 6:8; 1 Samuel 15:22; Ecclesiastes 12:13–14*

### SOMETHING TO TALK ABOUT

- How can we come to know what God requires of us?
- Are we told anywhere else, in detail, what it is that God requires of us?

### BIBLE READING: THE LORD REJECTS SAUL AS KING (1 SAMUEL 15)

- Why was God displeased with Saul, and what had Saul done?
- What did God say to Saul through Samuel because of what he had done?
- What do the words 'to obey is better than sacrifice' mean?

### ♫ Something to sing

May the mind of Christ my Saviour,
Live in me from day to day,
By his love and power controlling
All I do and say.

May the Word of God dwell richly
In my heart, from hour to hour,
So that all may see I triumph
Only through his power.

Katy B. Wilkinson (810, verses 1 and 2)

# 42

**Q** What rule did God first reveal to man that he should obey?

**A** The rule that God first revealed for man's obedience is known as the moral law.

*Romans 2:14–15; Romans 10:5*

### SOMETHING TO TALK ABOUT

- ◆ Why did God give man rules to follow?
- ◆ What happens if we disobey God's rules?

### BIBLE READING: SAMUEL ANOINTS DAVID (1 SAMUEL 16)

- ◆ Whom did Samuel anoint to be king in Saul's place?
- ◆ Why was he not chosen the first time when all the brothers gathered before Samuel?
- ◆ What does that teach us about God?

## ♪ Something to sing

Teach me, O Lord, your way of truth,
And from it I will not depart;
That I may steadfastly obey,
Give me an understanding heart.

In your commandments make me walk,
For in your law my joy shall be;
Give me a heart that loves your will,
From discontent and envy free.

The Psalter 1912 Alt (119F)

**43 Q** Where is the moral law summarized in Scripture?

**A** The moral law is summarized in the Ten Commandments.

*Deuteronomy 10:4; Matthew 19:17*

### SOMETHING TO TALK ABOUT

- How did God give the Ten Commandments to the people?
- Do you think the Ten Commandments are still necessary for today?

### BIBLE READING: DAVID AND GOLIATH (1 SAMUEL 17)

- Why was David sad that Goliath had not been defeated?
- Who was David really concerned about?
- What did David say to Goliath?

### ♪ Something to sing

Lord, make your Word my rule,
In it may I rejoice;
Your glory be my aim,
Your holy will, my choice.
Your promises my hope,
Your providence my guard;
Your arm my strong support,
Yourself my great reward.

Christopher Wordsworth (847)

## 44

**Q** What is the summary of the Ten Commandments?

**A** The summary of the Ten Commandments is to love the Lord your God with all your heart, with all your soul, with all your strength and with all your mind, and to love your neighbour as yourself.

*Matthew 22:37–40*

### SOMETHING TO TALK ABOUT

- ◆ Mention three ways in which we can show our love for God.
- ◆ Mention three ways in which we can show our love towards our neighbour.
- ◆ Mention three ways in which we can show our love towards ourselves.

### 📖 BIBLE READING: DAVID AND JONATHAN (1 SAMUEL 20)

- ◆ What was Jonathan's father's name?
- ◆ What sign did Jonathan give to David to tell him whether or not it was safe for him to come back to the place?
- ◆ Was it safe for David to return?

## 🎵 Something to sing ──────────────

We have not known you as we ought,
Nor learnt your wisdom, grace and power;
The things of earth have filled our thought,
Mere shadows of the passing hour.
Lord, in our minds the truth renew
And make us wise in knowing you.

Thomas B. Pollock (832)

## 45

**Q** What statement introduces the Ten Commandments?

**A** The statement which introduces the Ten Commandments is this: 'I am the LORD, your God, who brought you out of Egypt, out of the land of slavery.'

*Exodus 20:2*

### SOMETHING TO TALK ABOUT

- ◆ What does this statement tell us about God?
- ◆ What does this statement tell us about the children of Israel?

### BIBLE READING: DAVID SPARES SAUL'S LIFE (1 SAMUEL 24)

- ◆ Why was Saul chasing David?
- ◆ What could David have done to Saul?
- ◆ Why did he not take Saul's life?

### ♫ Something to sing

Infinite God, to you we raise
Our hearts in solemn songs of praise;
By all your works on earth adored,
We worship you, one true Lord;
The everlasting Father own
And bow our souls before your throne.

Charles Wesley (160)

## 46

**Q** What does the introductory statement to the Ten Commandments teach us?

**A** This introduction to the Ten Commandments teaches us that, because God is our Lord and our Redeemer, we must keep all his commandments.

*Deuteronomy 11:1; Luke 1:74–75; 1 Peter 1:15–19*

### SOMETHING TO TALK ABOUT

- Can we show our love to God by keeping some of his commandments?
- Do you think some commandments are more important than others?

### BIBLE READING: DAVID, NABAL AND ABIGAIL (1 SAMUEL 25)

- Who was Nabal?
- What did he do that made David angry?
- What did Abigail, Nabal's wife, do to stop David from coming to attack them?

### ♪ Something to sing

Jesus, Master, at your Word
We are gathered all to hear you;
Let our minds and wills be stirred
Now to seek and love and fear you;
By your teachings true and holy
Draw us, Lord, to love you solely.

Tobias Clausnitzer (556)

**47**

Q What is the first commandment?

A The first commandment is, 'You shall have no other gods before me.'

*Exodus 20:3*

SOMETHING TO TALK ABOUT

- ◆ Why are we to have no other gods?
- ◆ Can we serve God and something else at the same time?

BIBLE READING: DAVID AND MEPHIBOSHETH (2 SAMUEL 9)

- ◆ Who was Mephibosheth?
- ◆ Why did David want to be kind to him?
- ◆ How did David show him kindness?

♬ Something to sing —————————————————————

O worship the Lord in the beauty of holiness,
Bow down before him, his glory proclaim;
With gold of obedience and incense of lowliness,
Kneel and adore him; the Lord is his name.

J. S. B. Monsell (194)

**48**

**Q** What is required in the first commandment?

**A** The first commandment requires us to know and acknowledge God as the only true God, as our God, and to worship and glorify him.

*1 Chronicles 28:9; Deuteronomy 26:17; Matthew 4:10*

SOMETHING TO TALK ABOUT
- What does it mean to know God?
- What does it mean to worship God?
- What does it mean to glorify God?

**BIBLE READING: DAVID AND BATHSHEBA (2 SAMUEL 11)**
- Where should David have been when the events in this chapter took place?
- Why was it wrong for David to have taken Bathsheba?
- What did David do with Uriah, Bathsheba's husband?

♫ **Something to sing**

Great God of wonders, all your ways
Are matchless, godlike and divine;
And the fair glories of your grace
Among your other wonders shine.

*Who is a pardoning God like you,*
*With grace so free, so rich, so true?*
Samuel Davies (246)

**49**

**Q** What does God forbid in the first commandment?

**A** The first commandment forbids that we recognize any other gods as the true and living God and that we worship or serve them, for God alone is worthy to receive our worship and service.

*Psalm 14:1; Romans 1:20–21; Psalm 81:10–11; Romans 1:25–26*

### SOMETHING TO TALK ABOUT

- ◆ Why does God forbid the worship of other gods?
- ◆ Mention other gods that people worship and the way in which they worship them.

### BIBLE READING: NATHAN AND DAVID (2 SAMUEL 12)

- ◆ Who was Nathan, and what did he come to tell David?
- ◆ What was the story he told David that made David very angry?
- ◆ As a result of all this, what did David realize?

### ♪ Something to sing ────────────────

Lo, God is here; whom day and night
The choirs of holy angels sing;
To him, enthroned above all height,
Heaven's host their noblest praises bring;
Do not despise our humbler song,
Who praise you with a faltering tongue.

Gerhard Tersteegen, trans. John Wesley (240, verse 2)

**50**

**Q** What do the words 'before me' in the first commandment teach us?

**A** The words 'before me' in the first commandment teach us that God, who sees and knows all things, is very displeased by the sin of having any other god.

*Psalm 44:20–21; Romans 1:20*

#### SOMETHING TO TALK ABOUT

- There are two reasons given for not having other gods before God; what are they?
- Express these reasons in your own words.

#### BIBLE READING: SOLOMON ASKS FOR WISDOM (1 KINGS 3)

- Who was Solomon?
- What did Solomon ask God to give him instead of long life, wealth and victory over his enemies?
- What did God give to Solomon? (See verse 13.)

#### ♪ Something to sing

Eternal Light! Eternal Light!
How pure the soul must be,
When, placed within your searching sight,
It shrinks not, but with calm delight
Can face such majesty.

Thomas Binney (243)

## 51

**Q** What is the second commandment?

**A** The second commandment is, 'You shall not make for yourself an idol in the form of anything in heaven above or on the earth beneath or in the waters below. You shall not bow down to them or worship them; for I, the LORD your God, am a jealous God, punishing the children for the sins of the fathers to the third and fourth generation of those who hate me, but showing love to a thousand generations of those who love me and keep my commandments.'

*Exodus 20:4–6*

### SOMETHING TO TALK ABOUT

- ◆ What does this commandment teach us about worship?
- ◆ Does it tell us WHOM we are to worship or HOW we are to worship?

### BIBLE READING: SOLOMON BUILDS THE TEMPLE (1 KINGS 6)

- ◆ What did Solomon build for God?
- ◆ How would you describe the temple he built?
- ◆ How many years did he take to build the temple?

### ♫ Something to sing ───────────────────

Infinite God, to you we raise
Our hearts in solemn songs of praise;
By all your works on earth adored,
We worship you, the one true Lord;
The everlasting Father own
And bow our souls before your throne.

Charles Wesley, based on Te Deum Laudamus (160)

**52**

**Q** What is required in the second commandment?

**A** The second commandment requires us to accept and do all that God has said in his Word regarding religious worship, in a way which is pleasing to him.

*Deuteronomy 12:32; Deuteronomy 32:46; Matthew 28:20; Acts 2:42*

#### SOMETHING TO TALK ABOUT

- ◆ Can we worship God in any way that we wish?
- ◆ How do we know that our worship is pleasing to God?

#### 📖 BIBLE READING: THE QUEEN OF SHEBA VISITS SOLOMON (1 KINGS 10)

- ◆ In what city did Solomon build the temple?
- ◆ What did the Queen of Sheba come to see?
- ◆ Although Solomon was very wealthy, why did all the other kings come to visit him? (See verse 24.)

#### ♪ Something to sing

Search me, O God! My actions try
And let my life appear
As seen by your all-searching eye,
To mine my ways make clear.
Search till your fiery glance has cast
Its holy light through all,
And I by grace am brought at last
Before your face to all.

Francis Bottome (834, verses 1 and 3)

**53**

Q What does God forbid in the second commandment?

A The second commandment forbids the worshipping of God by the use of images, pictures or any other way not permitted (appointed) in his Word.

*Deuteronomy 4:15–19; Leviticus 10:1–2; Exodus 32:5, 8; Deuteronomy 12:31–32*

#### Something to talk about

- ◆ Why does God not allow us to make images or pictures of him?
- ◆ Can you think of other ways in which we should not worship God?

#### ✏ BIBLE READING: Elijah fed by ravens and the widow of Zarephath (1 Kings 17)

- ◆ Who brought Elijah bread and meat both in the morning and the evening?
- ◆ Why did Elijah leave and go to the woman at Zarephath?
- ◆ What did he ask this woman to do for him?

### ♫ Something to sing ───────────

O that the Lord would guide my ways
To keep his statutes still!
O that my God would grant me grace
To know and do his will!

O make me walk in your commands,
On this delightful road;
Nor let my head, or heart, or hands,
Offend against my God.

Isaac Watts (560)

**54**

**Q** What reasons are given for keeping the second commandment?

**A** The reasons given for keeping the second commandment are that God is the only one to be worshipped, that we belong to him, and that he will punish all those who do not worship him correctly.

*Psalm 95:2–3, 6; Psalm 45:11; Exodus 34:14*

### SOMETHING TO TALK ABOUT

- Why is God the only one to be worshipped?
- What will the punishment be of those who do not worship God?

### BIBLE READING: ELIJAH ON MOUNT CARMEL (1 KINGS 18)

- What was Elijah doing on Mount Carmel?
- What was the test that Elijah asked for, to see which god was the true God?
- What did God send at the end of the day in answer to Elijah's prayer?

### ♪ Something to sing

Before the Lord's eternal throne,
All nations bow with holy joy;
Know that the Lord is God alone,
He can create and he destroy.

Wide as the world is your command,
Vast as eternity your love;
Firm as the rock your truth shall stand
When rolling years have ceased to move.

Isaac Watts (208, verses 1 and 4)

## 55

**Q** What is the third commandment?

**A** The third commandment is, 'You shall not misuse the name of the LORD your God, for the LORD will not hold anyone guiltless who misuses his name.'

*Exodus 20:7*

### SOMETHING TO TALK ABOUT

- ◆ Why should we not take the Lord's name in vain?
- ◆ In what ways do people take the Lord's name in vain?

### BIBLE READING: THE LORD APPEARS TO ELIJAH AT HOREB (1 KINGS 19)

- ◆ Why did Elijah run away after all that happened at Mount Carmel?
- ◆ Do you think Elijah did the right thing to run away and hide?
- ◆ What was the prophet's name who took over from Elijah?

### ♫ Something to sing

How sweet the name of Jesus sounds
In a believer's ear!
It soothes our sorrows, heals our wounds
And drives away our fear.
                    John Newton (299)

## 56

**Q** What is required in the third commandment?

**A** The third commandment requires that we use God's names, qualities, words and works in a holy and reverent way.

*Psalm 29:2; Revelation 15:3–4; Ecclesiastes 5:1; Psalm 138:2; Job 36:24; Matthew 6:9; Deuteronomy 28:58*

### SOMETHING TO TALK ABOUT

- ◆ Mention one other name for God.
- ◆ Mention two of God's qualities.
- ◆ What are some of God's works?

### ◢ BIBLE READING: ELIJAH TAKEN UP TO HEAVEN (2 KINGS 2)

- ◆ Who was with Elijah when he was taken up to heaven?
- ◆ When Elijah came to the river Jordan, what did he do to cross over to the other side?
- ◆ How was Elijah taken into heaven?

### ♫ Something to sing ───────────────

Jesus is worthy to receive
Honour and power divine;
And all the blessings we can give
With songs of heaven combine.

Let all creation join in one
To bless the sacred name
Of him who reigns upon the throne,
And to adore the Lamb.

                    Isaac Watts (300, verses 3 and 5)

## 57

**Q** What does God forbid in the third commandment?

**A** The third commandment forbids using the name of the Lord for purposes other than worshipping God or acknowledging his power and authority.

*Malachi 1:6–7; Malachi 2:2*

#### SOMETHING TO TALK ABOUT

- ◆ When only is it right to use God's name?
- ◆ For what other purposes do people use God's name?
- ◆ What 'word' is used for taking God's name in vain?

#### 📖 BIBLE READING: THE WIDOW'S OIL AND THE SHUNAMMITE'S SON RESTORED (2 KINGS 4)

- ◆ What miracle did God perform through Elisha to help the woman pay her accounts?
- ◆ What kind deed did the Shunammite woman do for Elisha?
- ◆ What miracle did God perform through Elisha to help the Shunammite woman?

### 🎵 Something to sing ─────────────

Holy, holy, holy is the Lord,
Holy is the Lord God Almighty,
Worthy, worthy, worthy is the Lord,
Worthy is the Lord God Almighty,
Who was and is and is to come.
Glory, glory, glory to the Lord.

Anon (175)

**58**

**Q** What is the reason given for keeping the third commandment?

**A** The reason given for keeping the third commandment is that God's name is holy, and that he will punish those who use his name in a dishonouring way.

*Deuteronomy 28:58–59; Malachi 2:2*

#### SOMETHING TO TALK ABOUT

- ◆ What do we mean when we say, 'God is holy'?
- ◆ In what way will God punish those who use his name in a dishonouring way?

#### BIBLE READING: NAAMAN HEALED OF LEPROSY (2 KINGS 5)

- ◆ What was wrong with Naaman?
- ◆ To whom was he sent for healing?
- ◆ What was he told to do if he wanted to be healed?

#### ♬ Something to sing ────────────

Holy, holy, holy, Lord God Almighty!
Early in the morning our song of shall be;
'Holy, holy, holy; merciful and mighty,
God in three Persons, glorious Trinity!'

Reginald Heber (159)

**59** **Q** What is the fourth commandment?

**A** The fourth commandment is, 'Remember the Sabbath day by keeping it holy. Six days you shall labour and do all your work, but the seventh day is a Sabbath to the LORD your God. On it you shall not do any work, neither you nor your son or daughter, nor your manservant or maidservant, nor your animals, nor the alien within your gates. For in six days the LORD made the heavens and the earth, but he rested on the seventh day. Therefore the LORD blessed the Sabbath day and made it holy.'

*Exodus 20:8–11*

##### SOMETHING TO TALK ABOUT

* Do you think this commandment is important? Why or why not?
* To whom is this commandment given?

#### 📖 BIBLE READING: THE AXE HEAD THAT FLOATED (2 KINGS 6)

* What happened to one of the prophet's axe heads? How was it found?
* How would you describe this event?
* Why were the prophets cutting down the trees?

### ♪ Something to sing —————————————————————

Speak, Lord, in the stillness
Speak your word to me;
Hush my heart to listen
In expectancy.

Speak, O gracious Master,
In this quiet hour;
Let me see your face, Lord,
Feel your touch of power.

Emily M. Crawford (563)

## 60

**Q** What is required in the fourth commandment?

**A** The fourth commandment requires that we set apart the times that God has appointed in his word, specifically one day out of every seven days, as a day in which to worship him.

*Leviticus 19:30; Deuteronomy 5:12–14*

### SOMETHING TO TALK ABOUT

* Why is it important to have a set day in which to worship God?
* Mention two things that are important for us to do on that day.

### BIBLE READING: HEZEKIAH'S ILLNESS (2 KINGS 20)

* How many years did God give King Hezekiah to live after he had healed him?
* What sign did Hezekiah ask for to show him that God would heal him?
* What was the name of the prophet whom God used to speak to Hezekiah?

## ♪ Something to sing

Jesus, stand among us
In your risen power;
May this time of worship
Be a hallowed hour.
Breathe the Holy Spirit
Into every heart;
Bid the fears and sorrows
From each soul depart.

William Pennefather (228, verses 1 and 2)

**61**

**Q** What day of the week has God specifically set aside for man to worship him?

**A** From the time of creation, to the resurrection of Christ from the dead, the day of the week set aside by God was the seventh day, and since the resurrection it has been the first day of the week.

*Genesis 2:2–3; Acts 20:7; 1 Corinthians 16:1–2*

#### SOMETHING TO TALK ABOUT

- Does this mean that we are not to worship God on any other day?
- What is so important about the resurrection of Christ?

#### BIBLE READING: QUEEN VASHTI DEPOSED (ESTHER 1)

- What was the queen's name?
- What did she do that caused the king's anger?
- Do you think the king was right in doing what he did?

### ♫ Something to sing ───────────────

This is the day the Lord has made,
He calls the hours his own:
Let heaven rejoice, let earth be glad,
And praise surround the throne.

Isaac Watts (232)

**62**

**Q** How is the Sabbath day to be kept in a way pleasing to God?

**A** We keep the Sabbath day pleasing to God by resting from our normal worldly activities, those things which we do on every other day of the week, except those deeds of kindness which are necessary when it comes to helping others.

*Isaiah 58:13–14; Leviticus 23:3; Mark 2:27; Matthew 12:11–12; Exodus 16:25–28*

SOMETHING TO TALK ABOUT

- ◆ Mention two things that are usually done on other days of the week that could hinder our worship of God on Sundays.
- ◆ Mention some deeds of kindness that need to be done on Sundays.

**BIBLE READING: ESTHER MADE QUEEN (ESTHER 2)**

- ◆ Who was made queen in Vashti's place?
- ◆ What was her uncle's name?
- ◆ What great thing did he do?

**♪ Something to sing**

Jesus, I my cross have taken,
All to leave and follow you:
Son of Man, despised, forsaken,
Lord of all I am or do.
Perish every fond ambition,
All I've sought and hoped and known;
Yet how rich is my condition!
God and heaven are still my own.

Henry F. Lyte (843, verse 1)

# 63

**Q** What is forbidden in the fourth commandment?

**A** The fourth commandment forbids that we carelessly do the things that God requires of us, and that we do not use the day for doing those things which are unnecessary in thought, word or deed.

*Malachi 1:13; Ezekiel 23:38; Isaiah 58:13; Ezekiel 22:26; Jeremiah 17:24–26*

### SOMETHING TO TALK ABOUT

- ◆ How can we worship God carelessly?
- ◆ Mention two things that we often do on Sundays that are unnecessary.

### 📖 BIBLE READING: HAMAN'S PLOT TO DESTROY THE JEWS (ESTHER 3)

- ◆ Who was Haman?
- ◆ What did Mordecai do that made Haman angry?
- ◆ Haman developed a plan to deal with Mordecai and the Jews; what was it?

### 🎵 Something to sing ─────────────────────

Those who trouble and distress me
Drive me to your presence blessed;
Life with bitter trials may press me,
Heaven will bring me sweeter rest.
How could grief or sorrow harm me,
While my heart still feels your love?
How could this world's pleasures charm me
When you are my joy above?

Henry F. Lyte (843, verse 3)

# 64

**Q** What are the reasons given for the fourth commandment?

**A** The reasons given for the fourth commandment are that God has given us six days in which to do all our work, and he calls the seventh day to be a day of rest, in which to worship him, giving us his own example of resting on the seventh day and blessing it.

*Exodus 31:15–17; Leviticus 23:3; Genesis 2:3*

### SOMETHING TO TALK ABOUT

- ◆ Why did God rest on the seventh day?
- ◆ Is resting one day a week important? Why or why not?
- ◆ Remember those who have to work on Sundays and pray for them.
- ◆ What should people do who have to work on Sundays?

### BIBLE READING: MORDECAI PERSUADES ESTHER TO HELP (ESTHER 4)

- ◆ When Mordecai was upset, to whom did he turn for help?
- ◆ What did Esther ask Mordecai and the Jews to do?
- ◆ Why was Esther afraid to go to the king?

## ♪ Something to sing ───────────────

Take, my soul, his full salvation:
Conquer every sin and care,
Find in every situation
Joy and peace and service there.
Think what spirit dwells within you,
What a Father loves you yet,
What a Saviour died to win you:
Child of heaven, why should you fret?
                    Henry F. Lyte (843, verse 4)

## 65

**Q** What is the fifth commandment?

**A** The fifth commandment is, 'Honour your father and your mother so that you may live long in the land that the LORD your God is giving you.'

*Exodus 20:12*

SOMETHING TO TALK ABOUT

- ◆ Why do you think the commandment stresses 'fathers AND mothers'?
- ◆ Should parents expect children to do things which God's Word forbids?

**BIBLE READING: ESTHER'S REQUEST TO THE KING (ESTHER 5)**

- ◆ How did the king receive Esther?
- ◆ What did she ask the king to do?
- ◆ Haman was angry at Mordecai again and planned to do something to him. What was it?

♪ **Something to sing** ———————————

God of mercy, hear our prayer
For the children you have given;
Let them all your blessings share:
Grace on earth and joy in heaven!

In the morning of their days
May their hearts to you be drawn;
Let them learn to sing your praise
From their childhood's early dawn.

Thomas Hastings (932, verses 1 and 2)

**66** **Q** What is required in the fifth commandment?

**A** The fifth commandment requires us to honour, respect and obey our parents and to do the things that they require of us.

*Romans 12:10; Romans 13:1; Ephesians 5:22–23; Ephesians 6:1–2, 5*

### SOMETHING TO TALK ABOUT

- ◆ How do we honour our parents?
- ◆ How do we respect our parents?
- ◆ How do we obey our parents?

### BIBLE READING: MORDECAI HONOURED (ESTHER 6)

- ◆ Why did the king honour Mordecai?
- ◆ How did the king honour Mordecai?
- ◆ How did Haman feel about this, and why?

### ♪ Something to sing

Cleanse their souls from every stain
Through the Saviour's precious blood;
Let them all be born again
And be reconciled to God.

For this mercy, Lord, we cry;
Open now your gracious ear;
Since on you our souls rely,
Hear our prayer, in mercy hear!

Thomas Hastings (932, verses 3 and 4)

**67**

**Q** What is forbidden in the fifth commandment?

**A** The fifth commandment forbids our being disobedient and disrespectful to our parents, and not treating them in a way that is pleasing to God.

*Romans 13:7–8; Matthew 15:4–6*

#### SOMETHING TO TALK ABOUT

- ◆ Mention three ways in which we can be disobedient and disrespectful to our parents.

#### 📖BIBLE READING: HAMAN HANGED (ESTHER 7)

- ◆ What did the queen do at the meal?
- ◆ What did the king do when he heard?
- ◆ What did Haman do?

### 🎵 Something to sing

Our children, Lord, in faith and prayer
We bring before your face;
Let them your covenant mercies share
And save them by your grace.

In early days their hearts secure
From evil ways, we pray;
And let them to life's end endure
By walking in your way.

Thomas Haweis (933, verses 1 and 2)

## 68

**Q** What is the reason given for the fifth commandment?

**A** The reason given for the fifth commandment is the promise of a long life and God's blessing in the place where he has put us.

*Ephesians 6:2–3; Deuteronomy 5:16*

#### SOMETHING TO TALK ABOUT

- ◆ What promises are there in the first four commandments?
- ◆ What does the promise of 'long life and God's blessing' mean?

#### BIBLE READING: THE KING'S EDICT ON BEHALF OF THE JEWS (ESTHER 8)

- ◆ Who took the place of Haman?
- ◆ What did the king allow Mordecai to do?
- ◆ What did all the Jews do?

### ♪ Something to sing

We do not ask for wealth or fame
For them in this world's strife;
We ask, in your almighty name:
'Give them eternal life!'

Before them let their parents live
In godly faith and fear;
Then, Lord, to heaven their souls receive
And bring their children there.

Thomas Haweis (933, verses 3 and 4)

## 69

**Q** What is the sixth commandment?

**A** The sixth commandment is, 'You shall not murder.'

*Exodus 20:13*

### SOMETHING TO TALK ABOUT

◆ What does this commandment tell us about life?

### BIBLE READING: TRIUMPH OF THE JEWS (ESTHER 9–10)

◆ There was a great battle between the Jews and the rest of the people in the land. Who won?
◆ Because of the victory, they celebrated. What was the celebration called?
◆ Whose name is not mentioned in this book of Esther, and yet who controls all things?

### ♪ Something to sing ——————————

Boundless grace with you is found,
Grace to cover all my sin:
Let the healing streams abound;
Make and keep me clean within.
Living Fountain, now impart
All your life and purity;
Spring forever in my heart,
Rise to all eternity!

Charles Wesley (682, verse 4)

◆ Teach your family the Truth

**70**

**Q** What is required in the sixth commandment?

**A** The sixth commandment requires all lawful efforts to preserve one's own life and the lives of others.

*Ephesians 5:28–29; 1 Kings 18:4; Psalm 82:3–4*

#### SOMETHING TO TALK ABOUT

- Is all human life to be regarded as precious?
- How can we preserve our own life?
- How can we preserve the lives of others?

#### BIBLE READING: JOB'S FIRST TEST (JOB 1)

- Besides the angels, who else was in the presence of God?
- Who was Job?
- Why did Satan say that Job served God?

### ♪ Something to sing

Today your mercy calls us
To wash away our sin,
However great our trespass,
Whatever we have been;
However long from mercy
Our hearts have turned away,
Your blood, O Christ, can cleanse us
And set us free today.

Oswald Allen (677)

**71**

**Q** What is forbidden in the sixth commandment?

**A** The sixth commandment forbids that we should take our own life or the lives of others in an unlawful way.

*Acts 16:28; Genesis 9:6; Proverbs 24:11–12*

**SOMETHING TO TALK ABOUT**

- ◆ Why is it wrong to take one's own life?
- ◆ Is it ever lawful to take the life of another person?

**BIBLE READING: JOB'S SECOND TEST (JOB 2)**

- ◆ Why did Satan say that Job served God this time?
- ◆ What did God allow Satan to do this time?
- ◆ What did Job's wife say to him?

**♬ Something to sing**

My times are in your hand;
My God, I wish them there!
My life, my friends, my soul, I leave
Entirely in your care.

William F. Lloyd (765)

**72**

**Q** What is the seventh commandment?

**A** The seventh commandment is, 'You shall not commit adultery.'

*Exodus 20:14*

### SOMETHING TO TALK ABOUT

- ◆ What does this commandment protect?

### 📖BIBLE READING: JOB'S PROSPERITY RESTORED (JOB 42)

- ◆ What were the names of Job's friends?
- ◆ What did the Lord do for Job?
- ◆ After all that happened to Job, how much longer did he live?

### 🎵 Something to sing ————————————————

Shine now upon us, Lord,
True light of all today;
And through the written word
Your very self display,
So that from hearts that burn
With gazing on your face
Our children all may learn
The wonders of your grace.

John Ellerton (935)

**73** **Q** What is required in the seventh commandment?

**A** The seventh commandment requires us to keep others and ourselves sexually pure in our heart, in our speech and in our actions.

*1 Thessalonians 4:4; Ephesians 5:11–12; 2 Timothy 2:22; Ephesians 5:4; 1 Peter 3:2*

#### SOMETHING TO TALK ABOUT

- ◆ What can we do to keep ourselves pure in heart?
- ◆ What can we do to keep ourselves pure in speech?
- ◆ What can we do to keep ourselves pure in our actions?

#### BIBLE READING: THE WAY OF THE RIGHTEOUS AND THE WAY OF THE WICKED (PSALM 1)

- ◆ Which two people are described in this Psalm?
- ◆ What happens to them in the end?
- ◆ What does the 'law of the LORD' refer to?

#### ♪ Something to sing ————————————————

Live daily in us, Lord;
Your mind and will be ours;
You shall be loved, adored
And served with all our powers,
So that we all may teach
Our children, as they grow—
By something more than speech—
Your way, yourself to know.

John Ellerton (935, verse 4)

# 74

**Q** What is forbidden in the seventh commandment?

**A** The seventh commandment forbids any sexually impure thoughts, words and deeds.

*Matthew 5:28; Ephesians 5:3–4; Matthew 15:19*

## SOMETHING TO TALK ABOUT

- ◆ Why do we think impure thoughts?
- ◆ In what way can our words be sexually impure and displeasing to God?
- ◆ Is it right for a man and a woman to live together before they are married? Give reasons for your answer.

## BIBLE READING: THE SHEPHERD PSALM (PSALM 23)

- ◆ Who is David's Shepherd?
- ◆ Does David speak as though he is satisfied with his Shepherd?
- ◆ What are some of the things he says to prove it?

## ♪ Something to sing ───────────────

You I will love, my strength, my tower,
O Lord my hope, my joy, my crown:
You I will love with all my power
In all your works, and you alone;
You I will love until your fire
Fills all my soul with pure desire.

Charles Wesley (742)

**75**

**Q** What is the eighth commandment?

**A** The eighth commandment is, 'You shall not steal.'

*Exodus 20:15*

### SOMETHING TO TALK ABOUT

- ◆ What does this commandment protect?
- ◆ What does it mean to steal?

### BIBLE READING: GOD'S WILLINGNESS TO FORGIVE (PSALM 103)

- ◆ What does verse 1 tell us about David?
- ◆ What does verse 8 tell us about God?
- ◆ What do verses 15–16 tell us about man?

### ♪ Something to sing

My Jesus, I love you, I know you are mine;
For you all the pleasures of sin I resign:
To you, my Redeemer and Saviour, I bow—
If ever I loved you, my Jesus, it's now.

William R. Featherstone (735)

**76** **Q** What is required in the eighth commandment?

**A** The eighth commandment requires that we use only lawful ways in which to obtain and increase our possessions and the possessions of others.

*Proverbs 27:23; Acts 20:33–35; Philippians 2:4; Leviticus 25:35; Genesis 30:30; 1 Timothy 5:8*

### SOMETHING TO TALK ABOUT

- What are lawful ways of getting things?
- What are lawful ways of helping others to increase their possessions?

### 📖 BIBLE READING GOD'S ATTRIBUTES (PSALM 139)

- What do verses 1–6 tell us about God?
- What do verses 7–12 tell us about God?
- What do verses 13–16 tell us about God?

### ♪ Something to sing ————————————————

Be still, my soul, the Lord is on your side;
Bear patiently the weight of grief and pain;
Leave to your God to order and provide;
Through every change he faithful will remain.
Be still, my soul: your gracious heavenly friend
Through thorny ways leads to a joyful end.

Catharina A. D. Von Schlegel, trans. Jane L Borthwick (754)

**77**

**Q** What is forbidden in the eighth commandment?

**A** The eighth commandment forbids unlawfully taking anything that belongs to anyone else.

*Ephesians 4:28; Proverbs 21:6; Job 20:19*

#### SOMETHING TO TALK ABOUT

- What are the unlawful ways of getting things?
- Is it right to use unlawful means to get things in order to help others?

#### BIBLE READING: WISDOM'S REWARDS (PROVERBS 1–4)

- What is the beginning of wisdom and knowledge?
- Why are we told in Proverbs 3:5 not to trust in ourselves?
- What are we told to hold on to and to never let go of in Proverbs 4:13?

### ♫ Something to sing

Be still, my soul: your God will undertake
To guide the future as he has the past.
Your hope, your confidence let nothing shake;
All now mysterious shall be bright at last.
Be still, my soul: the winds and waves still know
The voice of Christ that ruled them here below.

Catharina A. D. Von Schlegel, trans. Jane L. Borthwick (754, verse 2)

## 78

**Q** What is the ninth commandment?

**A** The ninth commandment is, 'You shall not give false testimony against your neighbour.'

*Exodus 20:16*

#### SOMETHING TO TALK ABOUT

- What does this commandment protect?
- What does it mean to give false testimony?
- Who is our neighbour?

#### 📖 BIBLE READING: THE CALL OF WISDOM (PROVERBS 8)

- To whom or to what do you think the word 'wisdom' refers?
- What is better than gold? (See verse 19.)
- Who is the blessed or happy person? (See verse 34.)

### 🎵 Something to sing ————————————

Be still, my soul: the day is hastening on
When we shall be for ever with the Lord,
When disappointment, grief and fear are gone,
Sorrow forgotten, love's pure joy restored.
Be still, my soul: when change and tears are past
In his safe presence we shall meet at last.

Catharina A. D. Von Schlegel, trans. Jane L. Borthwick (754, verse 3)

**79**

**Q** What is required in the ninth commandment?

**A** The ninth commandment requires us to tell the truth at all times with regard to our neighbour, ourselves and to protect the reputation of others.

*Zechariah 8:16; 1 Peter 3:16; Acts 25:10; Proverbs 14:5, 25*

## SOMETHING TO TALK ABOUT

- ◆ What does the word 'truth' mean?
- ◆ How can we protect the reputation of someone else?

## BIBLE READING: THE PRINCE OF PEACE (ISAIAH 9)

- ◆ Who is referred to in verse 6?
- ◆ What are some of his other names, besides those mentioned in verse 6?
- ◆ When did these things take place?

## ♫ Something to sing ─────────────

My heart is full, O Christ, and longs
Its glorious subject to proclaim!
Of him I make my noblest songs—
I cannot cease to praise his name;
My eager tongue delights to sing
The glories of my heavenly King.

Charles Wesley (734)

**80 Q** What is forbidden in the ninth commandment?

**A** The ninth commandment forbids anything that would prevent the truth from being spoken or that would hurt anyone's name.

*Romans 3:13; Job 27:5; Psalm 15:3; Leviticus 19:16*

**SOMETHING TO TALK ABOUT**

- What should we do, if, to tell the truth, will mean some kind of trouble for us?
- What should we do if we hear someone saying something about someone else that is not true?

**BIBLE READING: THE SUFFERING AND GLORY OF THE LORD (ISAIAH 53)**

- Who is being referred to in this chapter as the one who suffered?
- When was this fulfilled?
- To whom does the word 'sheep' in verse 6 refer?

**♬ Something to sing**

Object of my first desire,
Jesus, crucified for me!
All to happiness aspire:
You alone our joy can be.
You to please, and you to know,
These are my delight below;
You to see, and you to love,
These are my delight above.

Augustus M. Toplady (738)

## 81

**Q** What is the tenth commandment?

**A** The tenth commandment is, 'You shall not covet your neighbour's house. You shall not covet your neighbour's wife, or his manservant or maidservant, his ox or his donkey, or anything that belongs to your neighbour.'

***Exodus 20:17***

#### SOMETHING TO TALK ABOUT

- ◆ What does this commandment protect?
- ◆ What is the meaning of 'to covet'?

#### 📖 BIBLE READING: THE IMAGE OF GOLD AND THE FIERY FURNACE (DANIEL 3)

- ◆ What did king Nebuchadnezzar make, and what did he command the people to do?
- ◆ What were the names of the three men who obeyed God rather than the king?
- ◆ What was their punishment?

### ♪ Something to sing ———————————

Loved with everlasting love,
Led by grace that love to know;
Spirit, breathing from above,
You have taught me it is so:
O what full and perfect peace,
Joy and wonder all divine!
In a love which cannot cease,
I am his and he is mine.
In a love which cannot cease,
I am his and he is mine.

George W. Robinson (715)

**82**

**Q** What is required in the tenth commandment?

**A** The tenth commandment requires that we are to be satisfied with all that we have in life and to respect the possessions of others.

*Hebrews 13:5; Romans 12:15; 1 Timothy 6:16;*
*1 Corinthians 13:4–7*

### SOMETHING TO TALK ABOUT

- ◆ Why should we be satisfied with what we have?
- ◆ Is it wrong to want possessions?
- ◆ If we want material 'things', what should we do about it?

### BIBLE READING: THE WRITING ON THE WALL (DANIEL 5)

- ◆ What happened during the feast that King Belshazzar had?
- ◆ Who was asked to explain the meaning of what happened?
- ◆ What was the meaning of this?

### ♫ Something to sing

My Jesus, I love you, I know you are mine;
For you all the pleasures of sin I resign:
To you, my Redeemer and Saviour I bow—
If ever I loved you, if ever I loved you,
If ever I loved you, my Jesus it is now.

William R. Featherstone (735)

## 83

**Q** What is forbidden in the tenth commandment?

**A** The tenth commandment forbids that we should be dissatisfied with anything that belongs to us or that we should envy the success of others or desire anything that belongs to someone else.

*1 Corinthians 10:10; Galatians 5:26; Colossians 3:5; James 3:14, 16*

### SOMETHING TO TALK ABOUT

- ◆ What happens when we covet what other people have?
- ◆ Can we be guilty of coveting only the 'things' that other people have?
- ◆ What should we do if we are guilty of coveting?

### BIBLE READING: DANIEL IN THE LION'S DEN (DANIEL 6)

- ◆ What command did King Darius give?
- ◆ Why did Daniel not obey the king?
- ◆ What happened to Daniel because of his disobedience?

### ♪ Something to sing

You I will love, my joy, my crown;
You I will love, my Lord, my God;
You I will love, beneath your frown
Or smile, your sceptre or your rod;
What though my flesh and heart decay?
You I will love in endless day!

Charles Wesley (742, verse 5)

# THE PENALTY OF BREAKING GOD'S LAW

**84** **Q** Can anyone keep the Ten Commandments of God perfectly?

**A** No. Since the fall of man in the Garden of Eden, no ordinary person has been able, or will be able, to keep God's commandments perfectly in this life, for they are broken daily in thought, word and deed.

*Ecclesiastes 7:20; Genesis 8:21; James 3:2, 8; 1 John 1:8, 10; Galatians 5:17; Genesis 6:5; Romans 3:9–21*

### SOMETHING TO TALK ABOUT

- Have you kept the commandments perfectly?
- What commandment did David break when he sinned in his relationship with Bathsheba?
- What commandment did Peter break when he denied the Lord Jesus?
- Who has kept the commandments perfectly?

### BIBLE READING: JONAH FLEES FROM THE LORD (JONAH 1–2)

- What did God tell Jonah to do?
- Was he obedient to what God said?
- What happened to Jonah because of the decision he took?

### ♫ Something to sing ───────────────

Finish then your new creation,
Pure and sinless let us be;
Let us see your great salvation
Perfect in eternity:
Changed from glory into glory
Till in heaven we take our place,
Till we lay our crowns before you,
Lost in wonder, love and praise.

Charles Wesley (714, verse 4)

**85** **Q** Are all sins equally sinful in the sight of God?

**A** All sins in the sight of God deserve death, but there are some sins which are more evil than others, because of the harm which comes from them.

*John 19:11; Luke 12:47*

### SOMETHING TO TALK ABOUT

- ◆ What is sin?
- ◆ Mention some sins that are more evil than others.
- ◆ What is the punishment for all sin?

### 📖 BIBLE READING: JONAH GOES TO NINEVEH (JONAH 3)

- ◆ What did God tell Jonah to do the second time?
- ◆ Was he obedient to what God said?
- ◆ What happened to the people of Nineveh?

### 🎵 Something to sing ───────────────

A mind at perfect peace with God;
O what a word is this!
A sinner reconciled through blood;
This, this indeed is peace.

Why should I ever anxious be,
When kept by power divine?
This is my God, who says to me
That all he has is mine.

Catesby Paget (713, verses 1 and 5)

**86** Q What does every sin deserve?

A Every sin deserves God's anger and punishment, both in this present life and in the life which is to come.

*Galatians 3:10; Matthew 25:41; Romans 6:23*

### SOMETHING TO TALK ABOUT

- ◆ Is God a God of love only?
- ◆ What is the difference between God's anger and ours?
- ◆ Name some instances in the Bible where God punished people for their sin.

### ▣ BIBLE READING: JONAH'S ANGER AT GOD (JONAH 4)

- ◆ What was Jonah's reaction to what God said?
- ◆ Why did he react this way?
- ◆ Was Jonah more concerned about people or plants?

### ♫ Something to sing

You souls redeemed with blood
And called by grace divine,
Walk worthy of your God
And let your conduct shine;
Keep Christ, your living head, in view
In all you say, in all you do.

Has Jesus made you free?
Then you are free indeed;
You sons of liberty,
You chosen royal seed,
Walk worthy of your Lord, and view
Your glorious head, in all you do.

William Gadsby (753, verses 1 and 2)

# HOW WE MAY BE SAVED FROM OUR SIN

**87**

**Q** What does God require of us that we may escape his anger and punishment that we deserve because of our sin?

**A** To escape the anger and punishment of God that we deserve because of our sin, God requires of us that we believe in the Lord Jesus Christ, that we repent of our sin, and that we carefully follow the instructions given in his Word on how to be saved.

*Acts 20:21; Proverbs 2:1-5; Isaiah 55:3; Acts 2:38*

### SOMETHING TO TALK ABOUT

- What other ways do people try and use to escape God's anger and punishment for sin?
- Is there any other way to escape God's anger and punishment?

### BIBLE READING: THE BIRTH OF JESUS (MATTHEW 1–2)

- What was so special and also so different about the birth of Jesus?
- What does the name Jesus mean?
- Why did Joseph and Mary flee to Egypt after Jesus was born?

### ♪ Something to sing

I am trusting you, Lord Jesus,
You have died for me;
Trusting you for full salvation
Great and free.

I am trusting you for pardon;
At your feet I bow,
For your grace and tender mercy
Trusting now.

Frances R. Havergal (698, verses 1 and 2)

**88**

**Q** What does it mean to believe in Jesus Christ?

**A** To believe (have faith) in Jesus Christ is a gift which God gives, which enables us to understand and receive the salvation that is in Christ alone and offered to us in the gospel.

*Ephesians 2:8–9; John 1:12; Philippians 3:9; Romans 10:14, 17; Galatians 2:16*

### SOMETHING TO TALK ABOUT

- Do we deserve this gift that God gives?
- To be saved, is it enough just to understand the salvation which is in Christ alone?
- What else do we need?

### 📖 BIBLE READING: THE BAPTISM OF JESUS (MATTHEW 3)

- What was the name of the person who was baptizing in the wilderness?
- Did he baptize everyone who came to him?
- What happened after Jesus was baptized?

### 🎵 Something to sing

I am trusting you for cleansing,
Jesus, Son of God;
Trusting you to make me holy
By your blood.

I am trusting you to guide me;
You alone shall lead,
Every day and hour supplying
All my need.

Frances R. Havergal (698, verses 3 and 4)

# 89

**Q** What does it mean to repent?

**A** To repent is a gift from God in which he enables the sinner, who has been made aware of his sinfulness, who has understood the salvation offered in Christ, who is sorry for his sins and hates them, to turn from them to God, with a desire to serve and obey him.

*Acts 11:18; Acts 2:37–38; Joel 2:12–13; Jeremiah 31:18; Psalm 119:59; Luke 18:13*

### SOMETHING TO TALK ABOUT

- Who makes us aware of our sinfulness?
- What does it mean to turn from one's sin?
- Why is repentance a gift from God?

### BIBLE READING: THE TEMPTATION OF JESUS (MATTHEW 4)

- Who led Jesus out into the wilderness to be tempted by the devil?
- What were the three different temptations that the devil used?
- Did Jesus give in to the temptations?

### ♫ Something to sing ───────────────

I am trusting you for power:
Yours can never fail;
Words which you yourself have given
Must prevail.

I am trusting you Lord Jesus:
Never let me fall;
I am trusting you for ever
And for all.

Frances R. Havergal (698, verses 5 and 6)

**90**

**Q** What are the ordinary, outward means that Christ uses to bring to us the benefits of salvation?

**A** The ordinary, outward means that Christ uses to bring the benefits of salvation to us are his Word, baptism, the Lord's Supper and prayer.

*Acts 2:41–42; 2 Timothy 3:15*

#### SOMETHING TO TALK ABOUT

- ◆ Mention some of the benefits of our salvation.
- ◆ What is the main benefit that the Bible gives to us?
- ◆ What is the benefit of prayer?

#### BIBLE READING: JESUS' SERMON ON THE MOUNT (MATTHEW 5–7)

- ◆ What are we, as Christians, to be in the world?
- ◆ What did Jesus say we are to do to our enemies?
- ◆ How many ways are there to get to heaven?

### ♪ Something to sing ─────────────────

By Christ redeemed, in Christ restored,
We keep the memory adored
And show the death of our dear Lord
Until he comes.

His body, broken in our stead,
Is seen in this memorial bread,
And so our faltering love is fed
Until he comes.

George Rawson (645, verses 1 and 2)

# THE BIBLE EXPLAINS THE WAY OF SALVATION

**91**

**Q** What makes the Word of God effective for salvation?

**A** The Holy Spirit of God makes the reading and the preaching of the Word the means to convince, convict and convert sinners (persuade them) to realize their need for Christ and to turn from their evil ways to God for salvation.

*Psalm 19:7; Acts 26:18; Romans 1:16; Romans 10:13–17; Acts 20:32; 2 Timothy 3:16–17*

### SOMETHING TO TALK ABOUT

- ◆ Why is it important to read God's Word?
- ◆ What is preaching? Why is it important?
- ◆ Can we be saved without the Holy Spirit?

### 📖 BIBLE READING: THE PARABLE OF THE SOWER (MATTHEW 13)

- ◆ What is the meaning of the word 'parable'?
- ◆ How many types of soil are spoken about?
- ◆ Only one type of soil produced a harvest that pleased God. Which one was it?

### 🎵 Something to sing

A debtor to mercy alone,
Of covenant mercy I sing;
Nor fear, with your righteousness on,
My person and offering to bring:
The terrors of law and of God
With me can have nothing to do;
My Saviour's obedience and blood
Hide all my transgressions from view.

Augustus M. Toplady (773)

## 92

**Q** How is the Word of God to be read, heard and applied for it to become effective for salvation?

**A** For the Word of God to become effective for salvation, we must listen carefully to it, prepare our hearts and minds through prayer to hear what it says, and we are to receive it with faith and love, hide it in our hearts and practise it in our lives.

*Proverbs 8:34; 1 Peter 2:12; Psalm 119:15; Hebrews 4:2; 2 Thessalonians 2:10*

SOMETHING TO TALK ABOUT

- ◆ How can we prepare ourselves to listen to the Word of God carefully?
- ◆ What does 'hiding the Word of God in our hearts' mean?
- ◆ How do we practise God's Word in our lives?

BIBLE READING: JESUS WALKS ON THE WATER (MATTHEW 14)

- ◆ What did Jesus do while his disciples were in the boat?
- ◆ How did Jesus manage to get to the disciples?
- ◆ What did Peter do when he saw Jesus coming towards them?

## ♫ Something to sing

How vast the benefits divine
Which we in Christ possess!
We are redeemed from sin and shame
And called to holiness.
Not for the works that we have done—
All these to him are owed;
But he of his electing love
Salvation has bestowed.

Augustus M. Toplady and Dewey Westra (711)

# BAPTISM AND THE LORD'S SUPPER

**93**

**Q** How do the ordinances/commandments of baptism and the Lord's Supper become an effective means of understanding the grace of God in salvation?

**A** Baptism and the Lord's Supper become an effective means of understanding the grace of God in salvation, not because of any special power in them or in the people who administer them, but only by the blessing of Christ and the working of the Holy Spirit in those who receive them by faith.

*1 Corinthians 3:7; 1 Corinthians 12:13; Matthew 3:11*

### SOMETHING TO TALK ABOUT

- What is the purpose of baptism and the Lord's Supper if they do not save us?

### BIBLE READING: THE TRANSFIGURATION OF JESUS (MATTHEW 17)

- Whom did Jesus take with him when he went up on to this high mountain?
- What happened while they were up there?
- Which two people from the Old Testament were also there?

### ♪ Something to sing

Move and activate and guide;
Varied gifts to each divide;
Gladly may we all agree,
Bound by loving sympathy,
Never from our calling move,
Needful to each other prove,
Kindly for each other care,
All our joys and sorrows share.

Charles Wesley (593)

## 94

**Q** What is an ordinance?

**A** An ordinance is a command given by the Lord Jesus Christ in which the work and the benefits of our salvation are presented and applied to believers.

*1 Corinthians 11:23–26; Genesis 17:7, 10*

### SOMETHING TO TALK ABOUT

- How many ordinances are there in the New Testament?
- Do these ordinances have any meaning for those who are not believers?

### BIBLE READING: THE TRIUMPHAL ENTRY INTO JERUSALEM (MATTHEW 21)

- Into which city did Jesus enter, riding on a donkey?
- What did the people do when they saw him coming?
- Who did the people think Jesus was?

### ♪ Something to sing

Sweet feast of love divine!
Your grace, Lord, makes us free
To feed upon the bread and wine,
Remembering Calvary.

Here every welcome guest
Waits, Lord, from you to learn
The Father's heart made manifest,
And all your grace discern.

Edward Denny (662, verses 1 and 2)

## 95

**Q** What are the ordinances of the New Testament?

**A** The ordinances of the New Testament are baptism and the Lord's Supper.

*Matthew 28:19; Matthew 26:26–28; 1 Corinthians 11:23–26*

### SOMETHING TO TALK ABOUT

- ◆ If an ordinance is a command of the Lord, do we, as believers, have the right not to keep them?

### BIBLE READING: JESUS ANOINTED, BETRAYED AND ARRESTED (MATTHEW 26)

- ◆ Who anointed the feet of Jesus with perfume?
- ◆ Who betrayed Jesus to the Chief Priests and for how much?
- ◆ What were some of the things that the people did to Jesus after he was arrested?

### ♪ Something to sing

My Lord, I did not choose you,
For that could never be;
This heart would still refuse you
Had you not chosen me:
You took the sin that stained me,
You cleansed and made me new;
For you of old ordained me
That I should live to you.

Josiah Conder (691)

# 96

**Q** What is baptism?

**A** Baptism is an ordinance or command of the New Testament, given by the Lord Jesus Christ, and is a public sign that the person baptized is in fellowship with Jesus Christ in his death, burial and resurrection, and it is a sign that his sins have been forgiven, and that he has given himself to God, through Jesus Christ, to live and to walk in obedience to him.

*Matthew 28:19; Romans 6:3–4; Colossians 2:11–12; Galatians 3:26–27*

### SOMETHING TO TALK ABOUT

- What does baptism show to people in the world?
- What can people expect of those who have been baptized?

### BIBLE READING: THE CRUCIFIXION (MATTHEW 27)

- Who sentenced Jesus to death?
- Who was released from prison in his place?
- Why did Jesus say, 'My God, my God, why have you forsaken me?'

## ♬ Something to sing

Unless your grace had called me
And taught my opening mind,
The world would have enthralled me
To heavenly glories blind:
My heart knows none above you;
For you I long, I thirst,
And know that if I love you,
Lord, you have loved me first.

Josiah Conder (691, verse 2)

## 97

**Q** Who, according to the Bible, should be baptized?

**A** Baptism is only to be given to those who have repented of their sins and come to faith in the Lord Jesus Christ.

*Acts 8:36–38; Acts 2:38–39; Acts 8:12*

### SOMETHING TO TALK ABOUT

- ◆ What does it mean to repent of our sins?
- ◆ What does it mean to have faith in Jesus Christ?
- ◆ Who are to be baptized: babies, adults or believers? Why?

### BIBLE READING: THE RESURRECTION (MATTHEW 28)

- ◆ After Jesus' death and burial, what happened on the third day?
- ◆ What were the guards who were watching over the tomb told to say?
- ◆ What did Jesus tell the disciples to do before he ascended to heaven?

### ♬ Something to sing

Jesus, how could I ever be
Ashamed of you, who died for me?
Ashamed of you, whom angels praise,
Whose glories shine through endless days?

Till then I'll boast of him who gave
His life my sinful soul to save!
May this alone my glory be,
That Christ is not ashamed of me!

Joseph Grigg and Benjamin Francis (637, verses 1 and 5)

**98**

**Q** How are believers to be baptized?

**A** Believers are to be baptized by immersion of the whole body in water, in the name of the Father, the Son and the Holy Spirit, according to the command of Jesus and the practice of the Apostles.

*Matthew 3:16; John 3:23; Acts 8:38–39*

SOMETHING TO TALK ABOUT

- ◆ What is the symbolism of being immersed in water?
- ◆ How were people baptized in the early Church?
- ◆ Who were baptized in the early Church?

**BIBLE READING: JESUS STILLS THE STORM (MARK 4)**

- ◆ What happened to the disciples that made them afraid?
- ◆ Where was Jesus at this time?
- ◆ What did Jesus do to take away the fear that the disciples had?

**♫ Something to sing**

Lord, make your Word my rule,
In it may I rejoice;
Your glory be my aim
Your holy will, my choice.

Christopher Wordsworth (847)

**99**

**Q** What is the responsibility of those who have been baptized?

**A** It is the responsibility of those who have been baptized to become members of the local Church of Jesus Christ and there to serve him using the gifts that God has given them.

*Acts 2:41–47; 1 Corinthians 12:12–30*

### SOMETHING TO TALK ABOUT

- ◆ Why is it important to belong to a church?
- ◆ How can we use our gifts in the church?
- ◆ Who suffers when we do not use our gifts?

### BIBLE READING: JESUS FEEDS THE FIVE THOUSAND (MARK 6)

- ◆ Why did the disciples want to send the people away?
- ◆ What did Jesus say to them?
- ◆ What did Jesus do?

### ♫ Something to sing ───────────────

Blessed be the tie that binds
Our hearts in Christian love;
The fellowship of kindred minds
Foreshadows that above.

We share our mutual woes,
Our mutual burdens bear;
And often for each other flows
The sympathizing tear.

John Fawcett (587, verses 1 and 3)

## 100

**Q** What is the Lord's Supper?

**A** The Lord's Supper is an ordinance or command of the New Testament given by Jesus Christ in which believers are given bread and wine that proclaim his death on the cross, and those who receive the Lord's Supper share, by faith, in all the benefits of Christ's death and become spiritually stronger in their Christian experience.

*1 Corinthians 11:23–26; 1 Corinthians 10:16; Luke 22:19*

### SOMETHING TO TALK ABOUT

- Why is it important for believers to have the Lord's Supper?
- Does the Lord's Supper have any meaning for unbelievers?

### BIBLE READING: THE RICH YOUNG RULER (MARK 10)

- What did this young man want from Jesus?
- Why do you think he came to Jesus?
- What did he have to do to receive what Jesus had to offer him?

### ♪ Something to sing

By Christ redeemed, in Christ restored,
We keep the memory adored
And show the death of our dear Lord
Until he comes.

His body, broken in our stead,
Is seen in this memorial bread,
And so our faltering love is fed
Until he comes.

The drops of his dread agony,
His life-blood shed for us, we see;
The wine shall tell the mystery
Until he comes.

George Rawson (645, verses 1, 2 and 3)

## 101

**Q** What is the correct way to receive the Lord's Supper?

**A** The correct way to receive the Lord's Supper is that those who receive it are to examine themselves, whether they correctly understand the meaning of Christ's death, whether they have accepted him as their Saviour and Lord, which will be seen in their repentance, love and obedience towards God, and his Word; otherwise they will be eating the bread and drinking the wine in a way that will not be pleasing to God.

*1 Corinthians 11:27–31; 1 Corinthians 11:18–21;*
*1 Corinthians 5:8; 1 Corinthians 10:16*

#### SOMETHING TO TALK ABOUT

- ◆ What are we to understand about the meaning of the Lord's Supper?
- ◆ What are we to understand by the words, 'examine yourselves'?
- ◆ Why is important to please God in all that we do?

#### BIBLE READING: THE GOOD SAMARITAN (LUKE 10)

- ◆ What two statements sum up the Law of God?
- ◆ What is so special about the Good Samaritan?
- ◆ What lesson is being taught in this parable?

### ♪ Something to sing —————————————

When I survey the wondrous cross
On which the Prince of glory died,
My richest gain I count as loss,
And pour contempt on all my pride.

Forbid it, Lord, that I should boast
Save in the cross of Christ my God;
The very things that charm me most,
I sacrifice them to his blood.

Isaac Watts (453, verses 1 and 2)

**102**

**Q** What do the words 'until he comes' mean when used in the Lord's Supper?

**A** The words, 'until he comes' plainly teach us that the Lord Jesus Christ will come a second time, and this is the longing of all believers.

*1 Corinthians 11:26; Acts 1:11*

#### SOMETHING TO TALK ABOUT

- ◆ Why is Jesus coming again?
- ◆ How is he going to come?
- ◆ When is he going to come?

#### 📖 BIBLE READING: THE PRODIGAL SON (LUKE 15)

- ◆ This chapter speaks about three things that were lost; what were they?
- ◆ What did the prodigal son spend all his money on, and what did he get in return?
- ◆ What did his father do for him when he returned home?

### 🎵 Something to sing ─────────────────

Lo! He comes with clouds descending,
Once for favoured sinners slain;
Thousand thousand saints attending
Hail the King who comes again.
Hallelujah! Hallelujah! Hallelujah!
God appears, on earth to reign.

Now redemption, long expected,
See with solemn joy appear:
Saints, whose faith this world rejected,
Meet their Saviour in the air.
Hallelujah! Hallelujah! Hallelujah!
See the day of God appear.

John Cennick and Charles Wesley (511, verses 1 and 4)

# PRAYER

## 103

**Q** What is prayer?

**A** Prayer is the offering of our praises to God, together with our desires, in the Name of the Lord Jesus Christ, for those things which are in agreement with God's will, confessing our sins and giving thanks for God's goodness to us.

*Psalm 62:8; 1 John 5:14; John 16:23; 1 John 1:9; Philippians 4:6*

### SOMETHING TO TALK ABOUT

- What four things are important when we pray?
- To whom do we pray?
- Why is it necessary to come to God in prayer through Jesus?
- Is there any other way of coming to God in prayer?

### BIBLE READING: THE STORY OF ZACCHEUS (LUKE 19)

- What kind of work did Zaccheus do?
- How do we know that he was saved?
- Why did Jesus come to this world?

### ♪ Something to sing ——————————————

Behold the throne of grace,
The promise calls us near;
There mercy shines in Jesus' face,
Who waits to answer prayer.
                    John Newton (602)

# 104

**Q** How has God taught us to pray?

**A** All Scripture is given to direct us in prayer, but we are specifically taught how to pray in the prayer which Jesus taught his disciples.

*Matthew 6:9–13; Luke 11:2–4*

### SOMETHING TO TALK ABOUT

- ◆ Do we need to be taught how to pray? Why?

### BIBLE READING: THE MIRACLE OF WATER INTO WINE (JOHN 2)

- ◆ Where was Jesus when he performed this miracle?
- ◆ What was the miracle and how did Jesus perform it?
- ◆ How do we know from this miracle that when Jesus does something, he does it perfectly?

## ♪ Something to sing ⎯⎯⎯⎯⎯⎯⎯⎯⎯⎯

Come, my soul, your plea prepare,
Jesus loves to answer prayer;
He himself has bid you pray,
Therefore will not turn away.

You are coming to a king;
Large petitions with you bring,
For his grace and power are such,
None can ever ask too much.

John Newton (603, verses 1 and 2)

# 105

**Q** What do the words 'Our Father ... in heaven' teach us?

**A** The words 'Our Father ... in heaven' teach us to come to God with confidence, remembering that he is holy and that he is willing and able to help us.

*Matthew 6:9; Isaiah 64:9; Luke 11:13; Romans 8:15*

### SOMETHING TO TALK ABOUT

- ◆ In the sense of saying, 'Our Father', of whom is God the Father?
- ◆ What does it mean to have a Father in heaven?
- ◆ When we pray, what are we to remember about God?

### BIBLE READING: JESUS AND NICODEMUS (JOHN 3)

- ◆ Who was Nicodemus?
- ◆ Why do you think he came to Jesus at night?
- ◆ What did Jesus say to him about eternity and the Kingdom of God?

### ♬ Something to sing

What a friend we have in Jesus,
All our sins and griefs to bear;
What a privilege to carry
Everything to God in prayer!
O what peace we often forfeit,
O what needless pain we bear,
All because we do not carry
Everything to God in prayer.
                    Joseph M. Scriven (614)

**106** **Q** What do we mean by the words 'Hallowed be your name'?

**A** By the words 'Hallowed be your name', we mean that God's name should be glorified, honoured and praised in all his dealings with men.

*Matthew 6:9; Psalm 67:1–3; Psalm 83; Romans 11:36*

### SOMETHING TO TALK ABOUT

- Why should God's name be glorified in everything?
- Who should glorify God in everything and why?

### BIBLE READING: JESUS AND THE WOMAN AT THE WELL (JOHN 4)

- Where did Jesus meet this Samaritan woman?
- What did Jesus say that he could give her?
- Where did the woman go to and what did she do when she left Jesus?

### ♪ Something to sing —————

Holy, holy, holy is the Lord,
Holy is the Lord God Almighty.
Worthy, worthy, worthy is the Lord,
Worthy is the Lord God Almighty,
Who was and is and is to come.
Glory, glory, glory to the Lord.

Anon (175)

# 107

**Q** What do we mean by the words 'Your kingdom come'?

**A** By the words 'Your kingdom come', we mean that God would destroy the kingdom of Satan, that God's kingdom would be established and advanced, that those outside of God's kingdom will be brought in, and that our Lord Jesus would come quickly.

*Matthew 6:10; Psalm 68:1; 2 Thessalonians 3:1; Romans 10:1; Revelation 22:20*

### SOMETHING TO TALK ABOUT

- ◆ How many kingdoms are spoken of in the Bible?
- ◆ How do we become members of either kingdom?
- ◆ Who is presently reigning over the world?

### BIBLE READING: LAZARUS RAISED FROM THE DEAD (JOHN 11)

- ◆ For how many days had Lazarus been dead before Jesus came?
- ◆ When Jesus told Martha that Lazarus would rise again, what did she understand that to mean?
- ◆ What did Jesus do to bring Lazarus back from the dead?

### ♪ Something to sing

Your kingdom come, O God!
Your rule, O Christ begin;
Break with your iron rod
The tyrannies of sin.

Where is your reign of peace
And purity and love?
When shall all hatred cease
As in the realms above?

Lewis Hensley (513, verses 1 and 2)

## 108

**Q** What do we mean by the words 'Your will be done on earth as it is in heaven'?

**A** By the words 'Your will be done on earth as it is in heaven', we mean that God, by his grace, would give us the desire and ability to know, obey and submit to his will in everything, as the angels do in heaven.

*Matthew 6:10; Psalm 119:34–35; Acts 21:14; Psalm 103:2–22*

### SOMETHING TO TALK ABOUT

- ◆ Can we do the will of God in our own strength?
- ◆ Why does God have to give us the desire to do his will?
- ◆ How do we show that we love God?

### BIBLE READING: THE ASCENSION OF JESUS (ACTS 1)

- ◆ What is meant by the ascension of Jesus?
- ◆ Who spoke to the disciples after Jesus had ascended to heaven?
- ◆ What was the most important thing that the angels said to the disciples?

### ♪ Something to sing

When comes the promised time,
The end of strife and war;
When lust, oppression, crime
And greed shall be no more?

O Lord, our God, arise
And come in your great might!
Revive our longing eyes
Which languish for your sight!

Lewis Hensley (513, verses 3 and 4)

**109**

**Q** What do we mean by the words 'Give us today our daily bread'?

**A** By the words 'Give us today our daily bread', we mean that God, by his grace, would supply our daily needs and that we may enjoy these blessings with contentment from him.

*Matthew 6:11; Proverbs 30:8–9; Psalm 90:17; Psalm 37:25*

### SOMETHING TO TALK ABOUT

- ◆ Why do we direct this request to God?
- ◆ Why are these needs spoken of as blessings?
- ◆ Why is it necessary to be satisfied with these things?

### BIBLE READING: THE COMING OF THE HOLY SPIRIT (ACTS 2)

- ◆ Who had promised that the Holy Spirit would come?
- ◆ How did the people know that the Holy Spirit had come?
- ◆ When the Holy Spirit came upon the disciples, what effect did this have on all the people who had gathered in Jerusalem?

### ♪ Something to sing

We thank you, then, our Father,
For all things bright and good;
The seed-time and the harvest,
Our life, our health, our food:
Accept the gifts we offer
For all your love imparts;
And that which you most welcome—
Our humble, thankful hearts!

*All good gifts around us*
*Are sent from heaven above:*
*Then thank the Lord, O thank the Lord*
*For all his love.*

Jane M. Campbell, based on Matthias Claudius (919, verse 3)

**110**

**Q** What do we mean by the words 'Forgive us our debts as we also have forgiven our debtors'?

**A** By the words 'Forgive us our debts as we also have forgiven our debtors', we mean that God, by his grace, and for the sake of Christ, would freely forgive all our sins and that he would enable us to forgive others.

*Matthew 6:12; Psalm 51:1, 7, 9; Luke 11:4; Matthew 6:14–15*

### SOMETHING TO TALK ABOUT

- ◆ Of what has God forgiven us?
- ◆ How did God forgive us?
- ◆ Why do we speak of God's forgiveness as a grace?

### BIBLE READING: PETER HEALS THE BEGGAR (ACTS 3)

- ◆ For how long had this beggar been crippled?
- ◆ What did he want from Peter and John?
- ◆ What did they give him instead?

### ♪ Something to sing

Depth of mercy! Can there be
Mercy still reserved for me?
Can my God his wrath forbear?
Me, the chief of sinners, spare?

Now, Lord, move me to repent,
Let me now my sin lament;
Now my proud revolt deplore,
Weep, believe and sin no more.

Charles Wesley (822)

**111** **Q** What do we mean by the words 'And lead us not into temptation but deliver us from evil'?

**A** By the words 'And lead us not into temptation but deliver us from evil', we mean that God would either keep us from being tempted to sin, or support and deliver us when we are tempted.

*Matthew 6:13; Matthew 26:41; Psalm 19:13; Psalm 51:10, 12; 1 Corinthians 13:10*

### Something to talk about

- ◆ Is temptation sin?
- ◆ Does God tempt people?
- ◆ Why does God allow us to be tempted?

### BIBLE READING: Philip and the Ethiopian (Acts 8)

- ◆ Where had the Ethiopian come from and where was he going?
- ◆ What was he reading, about whom was he reading, and did he understand what he was reading?
- ◆ Philip told him the good news about Jesus. What was this good news? Did the Ethiopian believe what Philip said?

### ♪ Something to sing

A sovereign protector I have,
Unseen, yet for ever at hand,
Unchangeably faithful to save,
Almighty to rule and command.
He smiles, and my comforts abound;
His grace as the dew shall descend,
And walls of salvation surround
The soul he delights to defend.

Augustus M. Toplady (774)

## 112

**Q** What do we mean by the words 'For yours is the kingdom, the power and the glory, for ever and ever, Amen'?

**A** By the words 'For yours is the kingdom, the power and the glory, for ever and ever, Amen', we mean that we recognize that God is our all-powerful King and that he is able to give us all that is good and that he is worthy of our praise.

*Matthew 6:13; Daniel 9:18–19; 1 Chronicles 29:10–13; Revelation 4:11; Revelation 22:20*

### SOMETHING TO TALK ABOUT

- Why is God worthy of our praise?
- Who alone is all-powerful?
- How has God shown us his goodness?

### 📖 BIBLE READING: THE CONVERSION OF SAUL (ACTS 9)

- What was Saul about to do when he was converted near Damascus?
- What were the first words that Saul said after Jesus said, 'Saul, Saul, why do you persecute me?'
- Who was Ananias, and what did the Lord tell him about Saul?

### 🎵 Something to sing —————————————————————

How good is the God we adore!
Our faithful unchangeable friend:
His love is as great as his power
And knows neither measure nor end.
For Christ is the First and the Last;
His Spirit shall guide us safe home:
We'll praise him for all this is past
And trust him for all that's to come.

Joseph Hart (788)

# Thematic index

While the following index is not comprehensive, it is intended to serve as a guide to the subjects—either mentioned specifically or referred to. The numbers following the subjects refer to the questions.

# About Day One:

Day One's threefold commitment:
- To be faithful to the Bible, God's inerrant, infallible Word;
- To be relevant to our modern generation;
- To be excellent in our publication standards.

*I continue to be thankful for the publications of Day One. They are biblical; they have sound theology; and they are relevant to the issues at hand. The material is condensed and manageable while, at the same time, being complete—a challenging balance to find. We are happy in our ministry to make use of these excellent publications.*

**JOHN MACARTHUR, PASTOR-TEACHER, GRACE COMMUNITY CHURCH, CALIFORNIA**

*It is a great encouragement to see Day One making such excellent progress. Their publications are always biblical, accessible and attractively produced, with no compromise on quality. Long may their progress continue and increase!*

**JOHN BLANCHARD, AUTHOR, EVANGELIST AND APOLOGIST**

Visit our web site for more information and
to request a free catalogue of our books.
www.dayone.co.uk

# Also available

## Lead your family in worship
### Discovering the enjoyment of God

FRANCOIS CARR

ISBN 978-1-84625-128-3

80PP, PAPERBACK

Every church and congregation wishes to experience growth: growth in membership, growth in church structures, growth in finances, growth in missionary and outreach programmes, as well as enjoying spiritual growth. Special projects, several methods, techniques and the attempts to transform communities are well known, but it seems that the implementation of these projects hasn't brought about a major breakthrough and any lasting and positive change in our society.

Churches consist of families ... and families consist of individuals. Few churches have focused their growth, and more specifically their spiritual growth, on the foundation of the righteousness and holiness of individuals and family membes. The root of healthy spiritual growth is the revival in the heart of an individul, a revival that has a clear impact on the family. If a family is spiritually healthy, it leads to spontaneous growth in the church and to spiritual development of the community.

'The Bible clearly instructs families to gather together for biblical teaching and worship. Francois Carr instructs most helpfully in great practical detail how each family can begin worship together in the home. I commend this awakening call with its clear instructions to the Christian public.'
**DR COLIN PECKHAM, FORMER PRINCIPAL, FAITH MISSION BIBLE SCHOOL, EDINBURGH, SCOTLAND**

'Probably one of the most neglected areas in Christian parenting is that of family worship. Francois Carr speaks to this subject that needs to be addressed in every Christian home and church. This book may sting with conviction, but I am sure it will encourage you in this most needy area of building Christian homes.'
**MARK D. PARTIN, PASTOR, INDIANA AVENUE BAPTIST CHURCH, USA**

'If there is to be revival in our lands and if there are to be great men and women of God leading our churches, then Christian parents must take seriously their calling to raise up a godly generation in their homes. This work will be a great help to those parents seeking to build homes that honour God.'
**DR RICHARD BLACKABY, DIRECTOR OF BLACKABY MINISTRIES, CANADA, AND AUTHOR OF SEVERAL BOOKS**